Explore! Theodore Roosevelt National Park

Help Us Keep This Guide Up to Date

Every effort has been made by the author and editors to make this guide as accurate and useful as possible. However, many things can change after a guide is published—trails are rerouted, regulations change, techniques evolve, facilities come under new management, and so on.

We would love to hear from you concerning your experiences with this guide and how you feel it could be improved and kept up to date. While we may not be able to respond to all comments and suggestions, we'll take them to heart and we'll also make certain to share them with the author. Please send your comments and suggestions to the following address:

The Globe Pequot Press
Reader Response/Editorial Department
P.O. Box 480
Guilford, CT 06437

Or you may e-mail us at:

editorial@GlobePequot.com

Thanks for your input, and happy trails!

Outfit Your Mind
falcon.com

A **FALCON** GUIDE ®

Exploring Series

Explore! Theodore Roosevelt National Park

A Guide to Exploring the Roads, Trails, River, and Canyons

Levi T. Novey

FALCON GUIDES ®

GUILFORD, CONNECTICUT
HELENA, MONTANA

AN IMPRINT OF THE GLOBE PEQUOT PRESS

A FALCON GUIDE®

Maps created by Trailhead Graphics © Morris Book Publishing, LLC
All photos by the author except where otherwise noted

Library of Congress Cataloging-in-Publication Data
Novey, Levi T.
  Explore! Theodore Roosevelt National Park : a guide to exploring the roads, trails, river, and canyons / Levi T. Novey. — 1st ed.

    p. cm. — (Exploring series) (A FalconGuide)
    Includes index.
    ISBN 978-0-7627-4087-1
  1. Theodore Roosevelt National Park (N.D.)—Guidebooks. 2. Outdoor recreation—North Dakota—Theodore Roosevelt National Park—Guidebooks.
I. Title.
    F642.T5N685 2007
    917.84'94—dc22   2007005096

Manufactured in the United States of America

Distributed by NATIONAL BOOK NETWORK

Contents

Acknowledgments

It was a dream come true to get to write a guidebook about one of my favorite places. It was a lot of fun—and a lot more work than I expected. Sometimes it was hard to make choices about what details to include, but as I heard a woman tell her son at a convenience store once: "If you can't decide what kind of candy you want, you're going to have problems in life!" Many people aided me in choosing the sweeter morsels of information to include in this book, as well providing countless suggestions for making it better. I would like to thank all of these people.

First and foremost, thanks to my friend Johnny Molloy for putting in a good word for me with the folks at Falcon and providing a less-experienced outdoor/travel writer with tips along the way. Expect a can opener in the mail soon, Johnny. Thanks to Scott Adams at Falcon for taking the chance on an unpublished author. I would like to thank Stephen Stringall for his help with the maps and Paulette Baker and Shelley Wolf of their production help.

Thanks to Wallace Dailey at Harvard University's Theodore Roosevelt Collection for aiding me with acquiring Theodore Roosevelt images. They really are important to the book. Thanks also to Marie Kutch and Dr. John Staudt of the Theodore Roosevelt Association for allowing me to use some of the information organized by the association in several places in this book.

In no specific order, I would like to tip my hat to all the kind, knowledgeable members of the Theodore Roosevelt National Park staff, including Bruce Kaye, Judie Chrobak-Cox, Todd Stoeberl, Beth Card, Taryn Flesjer, Darlene Lardy, Victoria Mates, Kane Seitz, Tom Cox, Susan Reece, Lynn Heiser, Mike Oehler, Laurie Richardson, and Valerie Naylor. Thanks to Jane Muggli of the Theodore Roosevelt Nature & History Association. The association runs the bookstores in the park's South Unit, Painted Canyon, and North Unit visitor centers, as well as the Knife River Historic Site bookstore, and uses the proceeds to support historical, scientific, and interpretive activities in the park. Thanks to Loren Yellow Bird for giving me an excellent tour and information about Fort Union Trading Post National Historic Site and Dorothy Cook for doing the same at Knife River Indian Villages National Historic Site. Thanks to Kevin and Beth Clyde for letting me stay above the Cowboy Cafe while doing my research.

Then, of course, I would like to thank the numerous friends and family members who gave me support and great ideas and proofread sections. I especially want to thank Marco Carbone, Peter Gleason, David Kurtz, Leo Lopez, Daniel Novey, Chris Novey, Edward Novey, and Ann Sibole for their extra efforts. Thanks to all the folks at Olympic National Park for showing so much enthusiasm for the book and toleration of my philosophical musings. A big hug and thanks to my wife, Alicia, for her endless support, unique perspective, and willingness to listen to me ramble on about ideas for the book.

One last thanks to all the teachers who have sparked my curiosity over the years, taught me a thing or two, improved my writing, and helped give me the confidence to do what I do. I'd liked to single out Alan Banks, John Brooke, John Carberry, Benjamin Dane, George Ellmore, Troy Hall, Sally Harris, Darcy Iams, Margaret Leary, Leigh MacKay, Richard Patterson, and Randy Reid.

Introduction:
One-of-a-Kind Journeys

Nestled within the western reaches of North Dakota, in a place sometimes known as "the badlands," a lesser-known national park awaits the lucky visitor. While many people arrive at this place not knowing much about it, the adventures, mysteries, stories, and beauty of Theodore Roosevelt National Park will often turn even the shortest visits into one-of-a-kind journeys. Will *you* make the journey?

We have Theodore Roosevelt to thank for many of the wonderful parks, forests, and special places that we have in the United States today. His adventures and experiences in the badlands served as a strong force, if not the primary catalyst, in making him want to preserve nature and our nation's historical sites. This quest was not only a personal one but also one that Roosevelt thought was in the best interest of all Americans. Today the man sometimes known as the "conservation president" has earned the distinction of being the only U.S. president to have a national park named for him.

The place where Roosevelt had some of his formative experiences as a conservationist awaits you. For people who choose to devote some of their time and interest, a wealth of discoveries and magic rests within Theodore Roosevelt National Park's boundaries.

Will this be you?

The Most Challenging Question

As a national park ranger, people often ask me, "Levi, out of all the parks you have worked in, which is your favorite?" Most park rangers who have worked for several national parks will tell you that "it depends," or that the answer depends on what aspect of a park you are talking about. I have worked as a ranger for six national parks and as a researcher at five others. I have also visited more than 100 of the 390 current National Park Service sites and countless national forests, state parks, county parks, city parks, wildlife preserves, and nature centers across the country. When I am asked which is my favorite park, I also avoid giving people a simple answer. But I'm going to let you in on a secret . . . Theodore Roosevelt National Park is always the first place that comes to my mind. Why?

The Ingredients for Success

Theodore Roosevelt National Park has all the right ingredients to make it one of the United States' future "destination" parks: a place not just on the way to somewhere else, but a place where people plan to end up. Divided into three units that total more than 70,000 acres, the park's scenic landscapes are home to an abundant variety of wildlife including bison, feral (wild) horses, prairie dogs, elk, coyotes, pronghorn, badgers, mountain lions, and golden eagles. Roads within the South and North Units of the park provide visitors with a means to get an excellent overview of the park's majesty. Of all the parks I have visited and worked in, I would rank this park second only to Yellowstone in the amount of wildlife that can be easily viewed (although I have never been to Alaska's parks, where animals also are abundant).

Ample recreation opportunities abound in the park and in nearby areas. These activities range from auto touring, hiking, camping, horseback riding, biking, canoeing, and bird-watching in the warmer months to exploring and cross-country skiing in winter. Almost 30,000 acres of the park are designated wilderness, making an appealing destination for those seeking fantastic hikes and solitude. You can hike anywhere you choose in the park.

As for ecological integrity, management, and gateway communities of the park, 300 park and conservation experts in a 2005 *National Geographic Traveler* survey ranked Theodore Roosevelt National Park as tied for eighth best among fifty Canadian and U.S. national parks. This survey was based on a stewardship index using a wide array of rating factors. The stunning scenery, wildlife, history, cultural resources, and recreation opportunities that Theodore Roosevelt National Park possesses make it one of the premier parks that has *yet* to be discovered by the masses.

How to Use This Book

As this is a guidebook, I encourage you to use it in the way that is most useful to you. You might choose to flip forward to those sections that interest you, or you might read the book from cover to cover. In either case, I hope that I satisfy your curiosities about this wonderful place. Before you continue, I want to give you an overview of the book's contents.

This book begins with a chapter that covers all the basic logistical information you will want to know about the park: where the park is located, how much it costs to enter, what times of year are busiest, some generalizations about the climate, and so on. The following chapter provides a biographical sketch of Theodore Roosevelt's life and accomplishments as a president and as a conservationist. I also will tell you about his experiences and adventures in North Dakota. The third chapter covers Medora, the park's primary gateway community. The town takes pride in its history and offers a wide array of entertainment, services, recreation, and lodging in the summer season. After this section, you can look forward to chapters about the diverse opportunities the park offers.

The heart of the book is organized into sections about the park's three units. While many similarities are shared by all three of these areas, each unit also has distinct features. For example, in the South Unit you have a chance to see wild horses. The North Unit contains several unique geological features, a historic demonstration herd of longhorn cattle, and a greater potential for a profound sense of solitude than the South Unit. The Elkhorn Ranch Unit allows the most passionate of Theodore Roosevelt (TR) enthusiasts to set foot where TR himself once pondered the beauty of the badlands. For these reasons, it makes sense to divide the core of the book into sections about each unit. Trails are generally described in these sections of the book and then detailed in the chapter about the park's backcountry: Walk Softly and Carry a Big Stick. Later sections discuss specific recreation opportunities such as biking, canoeing, and fishing, as well as nearby excursions and activities that might interest you. Additional information is located in the book's appendices. For fun, make sure to take the quiz about the park found in Appendix C!

As most visitors tend to visit only one unit of the park, the book is organized in such a way that I will always give general descriptions about specific park features, plants, animals, or stories in a sentence or two. If I elaborate more on such subject matter elsewhere in the book, the book's table of contents or index will tell you where it can be found. For instance, visitors to the North Unit will discover that the detailed discussion of bison—one of the park's most noticeable and intriguing animals—appears in the South Unit section.

As a final note, remember that we want future visitors to be able to see and enjoy the same landscapes, wildlife, plants, and history that we can experience today in this special place. Have a great time in the park!

The Maps

A FalconGuides® four-color fold-out map is provided at the back of this book. The front side of our map shows the park's South Unit with an accompanying map legend and a hypsometric key. Also on the front side is an overview map (inset) showing the park's three sections. The reverse side shows the park's North Unit with hypsometric key, map of the Elkhorn Unit (inset), and a locality map (inset).

The North and South Unit maps contain considerable detail, such as topography that shows both land and water features with the land elevation, measured in feet. In addition you'll find numerous activity icons on the maps highlighting visitor centers, hiking trailheads, overlooks, and canoe put-ins/takeouts, plus where to find prairie dog towns and a horseback-riding tour.

A few notes about reading the topography: All three unit maps plus the overview map use shaded, or shadow, relief. *Shadow relief* does not represent elevation. It demonstrates slope or relative steepness. This gives an almost 3-D perspective of the physical geography of a region and will help you see where the ranges and valleys are. The three unit maps also employ a technique called *hypsometry*, which uses elevation tints to portray relief. Each tone represents a range of equal elevation, as shown in the hypsometric key on the map. These maps will give you a good idea of elevation gain and loss. The color tones shown on the bottom of the key represent lower elevations while the tones toward the top represent higher elevations. Narrow bands of different tones spaced closely together indicate steep terrain, whereas wider bands indicate areas of more gradual slope.

If you'd like to supplement our maps with a more detailed map for back-country travel, you may want to obtain National Geographic's larger-scale map or you may prefer the 7.5-minute series of topographic maps published by the U.S. Geological Survey (USGS). Electronic versions of these maps can be found online or as packaged software. USGS maps are derived from aerial photos and are extremely accurate when it comes to terrain and natural features, but because the *topos*, as they are known, are not revised very often, trail, road, and other man-made features are often out of date. Even so, the 7.5-minute topo's fine depiction of topography is useful for seeing greater detail.

Basic Park Information

What can I see and do in the park? Theodore Roosevelt National Park contains fantastic scenery, a wealth of recreation opportunities, and an abundant amount of easily seen wildlife including bison, prairie dogs, and deer. The park also allows you to learn more about Theodore Roosevelt and how the time he spent in the region contributed to his development as a person and conservationist. The most popular activities visitors pursue in the park include auto touring, hiking, horseback riding, camping, and photography.

Where is Theodore Roosevelt National Park? Theodore Roosevelt National Park is located in western North Dakota, near the Montana border, in a region known as the Little Missouri Badlands. It is divided into three units: South Unit, North Unit, and Elkhorn Ranch. The entrance to the South Unit is in the town of Medora, off Interstate 94. The entrance to the North Unit is about 50 miles north of I–94 on U.S. Highway 85, about 15 miles south of Watford City. The Elkhorn Ranch is between the South and North Units and can make for an exciting half-day adventure.

What is the state of North Dakota like? North Dakota is a sparsely populated state with an economy based primarily on agriculture. The state leads the nation in production of durum wheat, barley, flaxseed, canola, oats, and many other crops. Most of the state has a flat landscape, with the

Badlands being a major exception. The state has a lot of wildlife and offers excellent opportunities for hunting and fishing. Theodore Roosevelt National Park is the state's major tourist attraction. More information about the state and its attractions can be found online at www.ndtourism.com or in the Nearby Excursions and Recreation Opportunities chapter. One last thing to note: The people you will meet in North Dakota are some of the friendliest folks you will ever come across.

What are "badlands"? Badlands are areas where erosion of the landscape has created a varied landscape, generally defined by buttes, gullies, and inconsistent vegetation. The area of North Dakota now known as the Little Missouri Badlands, or Little Missouri River Badlands, was first referred to by the Lakota people as *mako shika* (bad land). French explorers put their own spin on the name, calling the area *les mauvais terres à traverser* (bad lands to travel across). The name has more or less stuck. Today what you see in the badlands are colorful buttes and a varied topography that offer a stark contrast to the flat plains found in the adjacent areas of North Dakota and Montana.

Are the Little Missouri River Badlands the same as those in South Dakota? When most Americans hear the word badlands, they think of Badlands National Park in South Dakota. All "badlands" by nature have been shaped by the forces of erosion over time. In general, in the North and South Dakota badlands you can see many of the same species of animals and plants. But while there are similarities between the North Dakota and South Dakota badlands, there are also some differences. I personally think that the South Dakota badlands look at lot more like a desert, with little in the way of living creatures easily apparent. As a friend of mine says, "It looks like someone left the faucet on and everything washed away." I do not get that same feeling in the North Dakota badlands. North Dakota's badlands seem much more lush and full of life. While there are probably few black-and-white technical differences between the two areas, I have not heard many people argue that these areas closely resemble each other in appearance.

How can I get to the park? Most visitors drive to Theodore Roosevelt National Park. There is currently not much in the way of public transportation available. You can take a Rimrock Stage Trailways bus to Medora, but at that point you would have to walk or rent a bicycle to get around. Amtrak train service is available in Williston, about an hour north of the North Unit. The closest airports to the park are located in Dickinson (forty-five minutes east of the South Unit), Williston (one hour north of the

North Unit), Bismarck (two hours east of the South Unit), North Dakota, and Billings, Montana (four hours west of the South Unit).

Where can I stay? There are established campgrounds in both the South and North Units of the park. If you are looking for lodging or want to camp outside the park, Medora, Watford City, and other nearby areas have motels, campgrounds, and cabins. Refer to the Medora and the Camping, Lodging and Services chapters for specific information about where you can stay.

When is the park open? The park is open every day of the year. The park's visitor centers are closed on Thanksgiving, Christmas, and New Year's Day. In winter, the North Unit's visitor center is open on weekends and most weekdays. It is important to note that the North Unit is located in the central time zone and the South Unit is located in the mountain time zone. While visitor center hours vary, The South Unit is generally open from 8:00 A.M. to 4:30 P.M. in winter, with longer hours during summer; the North Unit is open from 9:00 A.M. to 5:30 P.M. Some portions of the park roads may close in winter due to snow or ice.

Are there better times of year to go? Most people visit Theodore Roosevelt National Park during summer and go to the South Unit. Conventional wisdom suggests that you should plan for your visit to occur sometime between late spring and early fall (May through September). Winters are cold but do not necessarily preclude a visit to the park. Summers can be very hot. At almost every time of the year (even summer), the park is not crowded. The park averages about 500,000 visitors each year—a very low number for a national park.

How much does it cost to enter? Check the park's Web site or call for current information about entry fees. Generally national park entry fees range between $10 and $20 per vehicle and are good for one week at all of a park's units. Camping fees are almost always an additional charge.

How can I contact the park? You can call, e-mail, or write the park for more information. Numbers and addresses are:
South Unit: (701) 623–4466
North Unit: (701) 842–2333
Address: Theodore Roosevelt National Park, Box 7, Medora,
          ND 58645-0007

Does the park have an Internet site? Yes. The park has an excellent Web site with loads of information: www.nps.gov/thro.

Theodore Roosevelt— Man of Action

If Theodore Roosevelt were living today, he would probably want to play himself in a movie about his life. Imagine standing in line to buy a ticket thinking, "Who better to play Roosevelt than Roosevelt?" He was, after all, one of the superb actors of his time.

Roosevelt was an actor in two senses: His popularity, accomplishments, and intriguing life were the products of a serious effort on his part to cultivate a dynamic private and public self-image. This image provided him with the power to act with great effectiveness as the country's chief executive. While he was at times inconsistent, his ability to transcend his wealthy Harvard-educated background and strong opinions made him likable to most people, and they came to believe in him as a person who could lead the nation to greatness. Among his many accomplishments, most historians consider Roosevelt's contributions to conservation to be his most enduring achievement as president.

How Roosevelt Became President

John Adams popularized a belief that the vice presidency was "the most insignificant office that ever the invention of man contrived or his imagination conceived." Adams was articulating a view held by some of his contemporaries that the American vice president had so little power that the position was virtually worthless. Through his work, involvement, and resolve in New York and national politics in the late 1890s, Theodore Roosevelt would become so annoying to other politicians that they winked to one another and made him the vice presidential candidate for the Republican ticket. In 1900 William McKinley won his second term as president, with Roosevelt now his second in command. By this time Roosevelt had already written several books and been governor of New York, New York City police commissioner, assistant secretary of the Navy, cowboy, rancher, and an Army colonel who had led the "Rough Riders" to a celebrated victory in the Spanish-American War. His wealth of experiences prepared him for a destiny that would go beyond the office of vice president. When President McKinley was assassinated by an anarchist in 1901, just nine months into his second term, Roosevelt became the new president.

Roosevelt was the youngest president in American history, taking office at the age of forty-two, and quickly became involved in a wide variety of pursuits. Countless biographies have chronicled various aspects of Roosevelt's life and presidency. To provide you with a short explanation of the "greatest hits," one must start with Roosevelt's reputation as a "trust buster." Starting with a growing monopoly of railroad companies, the Northern Securities Company, Roosevelt began orchestrating antitrust regulations that provided at least symbolic consumer and federal protection from private economic interests. These actions added to his popularity among most Americans. Roosevelt also took personal interest in checking the growth of other huge business groups, including oil and tobacco companies. Roosevelt argued that "there is a widespread conviction in the minds of the American people that the great corporations known as trusts are in certain of their features and tendencies hurtful to the general welfare . . . Corporations engaged in interstate commerce should be regulated if they are found to exercise a license working to public injury."

Roosevelt actually supported big business more than might seem apparent. He distinguished between "good" and "bad" trusts. He knew that to be an effective president, he would have to have some friends in high places. Acting once again, Roosevelt would enjoy a public reputation as a trust

Ten Fascinating Facts about Theodore Roosevelt

Theodore Roosevelt . . .

- Conserved an estimated 230 million acres of land by designating areas as national forests, national parks, bird preserves, and wildlife preserves.
- Negotiated the end to the Russo-Japanese War and for his efforts won the Nobel Peace Prize.
- Was the first U.S. president to fly in an airplane, ride in a submarine, own a car, and travel outside the country while president.
- Was the presidential candidate of the Progressive Party (also known as the Bull Moose party) in 1912 and is the only third-party candidate to have ever come in second in voting totals. (He beat the incumbent, William Howard Taft, but lost to Woodrow Wilson.)
- Was the primary architect of a war for independence in a province of Colombia just so that the Panama Canal could be built.
- Helped initiate the dialogue that would create the National Collegiate Athletic Association (NCAA) and change the rules of football so that it would be a less-deadly sport. (Many people wanted football to be banned because it was such a violent sport. Eighteen players died in 1905 alone!)
- Was the first U.S. president to be filmed extensively. (You can see the films online at www.memory.loc.gov/ammem/collections/troosevelt_film.)
- Was the first president to be commonly known by his initials: TR.
- Inspired the "teddy bear" but hated being called Teddy.
- Drank about a gallon of coffee per day!

Some of this information was provided courtesy of The Theodore Roosevelt Association; P.O. Box 719, Oyster Bay, NY 11771; www.theodoreroosevelt.org.

buster while patting the backs of his big-business buddies in less visible places.

Roosevelt also discovered a loophole in federal laws and unilaterally began to designate massive amounts of land as protected areas—much to the chagrin of other politicians who preferred that Roosevelt work with Congress to pursue a more conservative agenda. During his presidency 150 national forests, 51 bird preserves, 18 national monuments, 5 national parks, and 4 wildlife preserves were created. While other individuals might have contributed more of the philosophical grounds for conservation, Roosevelt was the person who is largely responsible for enacting the legislation that protected extensive amounts of areas and resources. *National Geographic* estimates that during his presidency 230 million acres of land were protected.

In 1907 Roosevelt remarked that "the conservation of natural resources is the fundamental problem. Unless we solve that problem it will avail us little to solve all others." In that same year he added, "Optimism is a good characteristic, but if carried to an excess, it becomes foolishness. We are prone to speak of the resources of this country as inexhaustible; this is not so." Three years later, Roosevelt clarified his stance: "The object of government is the welfare of the people. . . . Conservation means development as much as it does protection. I recognize the right and duty of this generation to develop and use the natural resources of our land; but I do not recognize the right to waste them, or to rob, by wasteful use, the generations that come after us." He lobbied this idea even after his presidency, stating that "there can be no greater issue than that of conservation in this country."

Roosevelt launched numerous conservation commissions, clubs, and conferences. He also appointed Gifford Pinchot as the chief of the Forest Service and conferred with many of the leading conservationists of his time. For his conservation accomplishments, he is often referred to as America's "Conservation President." Places that Roosevelt designated as protected areas are listed in Appendix A of this book. Some of the more well-known places include Mesa Verde National Park, Grand Canyon National Monument (which later became a national park), Devils Tower National Monument, and Olympic National Monument (which later became a national park).

Roosevelt's presidential influence was not limited to antitrust regulations and conservation. He also wanted to show the rest of the world the rising power of the United States and was extremely active in global affairs. He sent the battleships of the U.S. Navy, known as the "Great White Fleet" around the world for two years to provide a spectacle of military power. He wanted to build the Panama Canal so badly that he helped engineer a revolution in Panama (which at the time was a province of the Colombian government) to secure American interests in the region. In addition, Roosevelt

Theodore Roosevelt, one of the most influential presidents in American history, involved himself with regulation of big businesses, labor laws, conservation, and international affairs.
THEODORE ROOSEVELT COLLECTION, HARVARD COLLEGE LIBRARY.

won the Nobel Peace Prize for successfully mediating an end to the Russo-Japanese War.

Roosevelt was also generally a champion of child labor laws and supported most labor strikes and a worker's right to a living wage. He was a supporter of women's suffrage and the women's rights movement. He enacted laws that regulated the nation's food and drug industries after reading Upton Sinclair's *The Jungle* (an account of the failings and unsanitary conditions of Chicago's meatpacking plants) and reformed the rules of foot-

Origin of the Teddy Bear

Did you know that Theodore Roosevelt inspired the teddy bear? In 1902 Roosevelt went on a hunting trip in Mississippi hoping to kill a bear. His guides wanted him to succeed and on the fourth day found an old bear for Roosevelt to kill. Roosevelt refused on principle to shoot such a weakened beast for sport. The story spread, and a cartoonist named Clifford Berryman depicted the event in a newspaper. Many future cartoons included Roosevelt with the bear. A toy store owner named Morris Michtom came up with a clever idea after seeing the cartoon. He took several stuffed bears his wife had made and asked Roosevelt permission to call them "Teddy's Bears." The idea took off, and the teddy bear was born!

ball while helping to set up the National Collegiate Athletic Association (NCAA).

Roosevelt remained quite active after his presidency. He went to Africa with his son to hunt and obtain specimens for the Smithsonian's collection. Another event of interest was his run as a third-party candidate in 1912 for the Progressive Party (or "Bull Moose" party). Roosevelt decided to run again after his friend and groomed presidential successor, William Howard Taft, strayed from his political advice and desires. Roosevelt beat Taft at the polls but came in second to Woodrow Wilson.

Roosevelt later went to South America on a lecture tour. During this tour he joined a very dangerous expedition through the "uncharted" Amazon region of South America on the River of Doubt. He became sick on the perilous journey and nearly died from malaria and dysentery.

At the outbreak of World War I, Roosevelt desperately wanted the United States to take action, but President Woodrow Wilson instead chose to do little. Roosevelt witnessed his brand of "imperialist" politics being replaced by a policy of neutrality. Once the United States finally entered the war in 1917, Roosevelt implored Wilson to let him lead a regiment of soldiers into France. Wilson turned him down, as Roosevelt had been a critical thorn throughout Wilson's presidency.

Roosevelt died just two years later, at the age of sixty. As president he led the United States through a period of political and social transition and greatly increased the executive powers of the president. His ability to act with confidence as president was possible because of his popularity and superb ability to act as the protector and benefactor of the American people. Nonetheless, he believed that the president should be held as accountable as possible by the American people.

About seven months before his death, Roosevelt said,

> "The President is merely the most important among a large number of public servants. He should be supported or opposed exactly to the degree which is warranted by his good conduct or bad conduct, his efficiency or inefficiency in rendering loyal, able, and disinterested service to the Nation as a whole. Therefore it is absolutely necessary that there should be full liberty to tell the truth about his acts, and this means that it is exactly necessary to blame him when he does wrong as to praise him when he does right. Any other attitude in an American citizen is both base and servile. To announce that there must be no criticism of the President, or that we are to stand by the President, right or wrong, is not only unpatriotic and servile, but is morally treasonable to the American public. Nothing but the truth should be spoken about him or any one else. But it is even more important to tell the truth, pleasant or unpleasant, about him than about any one else."

As a visitor to Theodore Roosevelt National Park, you undoubtedly want to know more about Roosevelt's experiences in the badlands. Roosevelt journeyed to the Dakota Territory in 1883 at the age of twenty-four to hunt bison. While Roosevelt arrived inexperienced, he had some fundamental confidence-building experiences in the badlands that would change him. He would later claim, "I would not have been President had it not been for my experience in the Dakota Territory."

Roosevelt in the Little Missouri River Badlands

Roosevelt initially headed west because of word-of-mouth and newspaper accounts about the good hunting to be found in the Little Missouri River Badlands. He wanted to hunt bison and also see the American frontier. His heart set, Roosevelt took a train out to the young town of Little Missouri and hired Joe Ferris to serve as his hunting guide. Ferris and Roosevelt searched unsuccessfully for more than a week before finally finding a bison for Roosevelt to shoot. After one rainy night during the hunt, Roosevelt and Ferris woke up in about 4 inches of water. Ferris shared his discomfort with

Roosevelt (on the left) journeyed to North Dakota to hunt bison and totally immersed himself in the culture of the American West. THEODORE ROOSEVELT COLLECTION, HARVARD COLLEGE LIBRARY.

Roosevelt in coarse words, but an enthusiastic Roosevelt replied to Ferris, "By Godfrey, but this is fun!" Ferris was impressed by Roosevelt's determination on the hunt, despite the rough conditions and Roosevelt's lack of experience.

Roosevelt enjoyed conversing with locals and cattle ranchers during his visit and was apparently such a lively debater of politics that he would often sit in rocking chairs and rock himself across the room. He decided that being a cattle rancher might be profitable and bought out two of the partners in the Maltese Cross Cattle Ranch (also sometimes known as the Chimney Butte Ranch). Roosevelt's partners, Sylvane Ferris (Joe Ferris's brother) and William Merrifield, operated the ranch. He soon established another ranch, known as the Elkhorn, and hired two friends from Maine, Bill Sewall and Wilmot Dow, to run it. Having others take care of his ranches freed Roosevelt to come and go as he pleased—living the life of cowboy and the life of an elite Eastern politician at the same time.

On February 12, 1884, Theodore Roosevelt's first child was born. Two days later, on Valentine's Day, both his wife and mother died. Following a political defeat that spring, Roosevelt retreated to the Dakota Territory to heal and take a break from politics, leaving his child with his sister, Bamie. It was during this substantial time in the Dakota Territory that Roosevelt began to understand people not like himself, relate to them, and also assert his strength of character. It was a key period in Roosevelt's life.

According to a famous legend from this period, one night Roosevelt entered a saloon in the town of Mingusville (now Wibaux, Montana). A man in the bar shouted that "Four Eyes is going to treat." There was some nervous laughter in the room, and Roosevelt tried to ignore the request. The bar bully walked over to Roosevelt, held two guns on him, and reiterated his desire that the man wearing glasses buy the bar a round. Roosevelt later claimed this was a moment of truth that would forever mark his reputation in the West. He responded with a swift right to the bully's face, followed by a couple more blows. As the man went down, he fired both guns, the bullets spreading wide of Roosevelt. The bully's friends saved him further embarrassment and dragged him outside. Roosevelt sat down and then ate dinner from a corner view, no doubt rattled but proud of himself. Word spread across the region of Roosevelt's bar brawl. From then on he was known, respectfully, as "Old Four Eyes."

Roosevelt sparred with the less law-abiding citizens of Medora on numerous occasions, and eventually some of his friends formed a coalition to help protect the rights of ranchers and provide some semblance of civil order. Roosevelt was elected chairman and also wrote the constitution for what became known as the Little Missouri Stockmen's Association. The formation of this organization marked a transition in the Medora area toward more law and order. Other factors, however, would make Roosevelt's time as a rancher relatively short.

The winter of 1886–87 was harsh and affected almost all cattle ranchers in the West. Most ranchers, Roosevelt included, lost a significant amount of their cattle to cold temperatures and lack of vegetation. Roosevelt slowly began to cut his losses and in several years would sell the rights to both of his ranches. He made his final trip to the Medora area in 1911.

While Roosevelt was in North Dakota, his attitudes toward conservation were strongly influenced by the uncontrolled overgrazing of range he witnessed and also by the plight of wildlife like bison. Late in his life as president, Roosevelt created the National Bison Refuge to help protect the animals. He had earlier helped form a wildlife conservation group, known as the Boone and Crockett Club.

Shortly after Roosevelt died in 1919, efforts commenced to create a memorial park in the badlands that would honor the late president. In 1946 part of the area was designated a national wildlife refuge. The refuge plus the Elkhorn Ranch became a memorial park in 1947. The North Unit was added in 1948, and the park was designated by Congress as Theodore Roosevelt National Park in 1978.

Stories about Roosevelt in the badlands are sprinkled throughout the rest of this book. Check the Visiting Elkhorn Ranch chapter for the most information. For more information about books and Web sites on Roosevelt's life, see Appendix A: Additional Resources.

Medora:
Gateway to the South Unit

Many national parks have nearby towns or cities that are referred to as "gateway communities." To visit some parks, you will often have to drive through these communities to reach an entrance. Medora is the primary gateway community for Theodore Roosevelt National Park, and it takes advantage of its legitimate connections to cowboys, gunslingers, and Theodore Roosevelt to make an experience that is in harmony with the park.

In summer there are a lot of things to do in Medora. (In other times of the year, the pace slows considerably.) There are plenty of places to stay, camp, shop, and eat in Medora. Almost any place you go in Medora, you can get a free map, so don't worry too much about getting around. Almost everything in Medora is within a 0.25-mile radius. For nightlife, the famous Pitchfork Fondue and the Medora Musical are experiences that should not be missed if you have the time. But before I describe all the options Medora offers, I want to tell you a little bit more about the town's history.

A Wild West Town

The story of Medora begins with hostilities between the Lakota and the U.S. government starting in the 1850s. The U.S. government was forcing many American Indian tribes onto reservations during this period, and the Lakota, like many other tribes, were fighting to maintain their autonomy. U.S. Army expeditions made their way through North Dakota hoping to force various bands of the Lakota onto reservations. The struggle would continue for many years. As the Sioux and other tribes were pushed farther west, they began to attack the most visible symbol and tool that allowed white settlers to expand into Indian territory: railroads. The army began to help protect railroad crews from Indian attacks. A military cantonment was established in 1879 on the west side of the Little Missouri River to provide protection for the Northern Pacific Railroad as it laid tracks west of that point. The town of Little Missouri was created nearby by entrepreneurs to supply soldiers and frontiersmen with goods and entertainment.

People in Little Missouri began to appreciate the abundance of wildlife in the badlands area and began to advertise hunting guide services. A hotel was built to serve as a departure point for tourists. Word spread quickly about the great hunting offered in the Dakota Territory, attracting the two people who were most influential to the Medora area's history. As discussed in the previous chapter, Theodore Roosevelt came to the area in the fall of 1883 to hunt bison and soon thereafter decided to enter the cattle business. The other important individual was a French aristocrat, the Marquis de Mores. The marquis was by all accounts an arrogant man who had a wealth of eccentric and curious ideas about how to make his fortune. He also had the financial backing of his family to play with. He came to Little Missouri in the spring of 1883 and decided to construct a new town directly across the Little Missouri River. He named the town for his wife, Medora. After deciding to create Medora, the marquis constructed a large house for his family and built a beef packing plant. His plan was to ship meat directly to Eastern cities via refrigerated train cars. While the marquis actually had some good business ideas, he was not good at managing his business ventures. The marquis's money-making scheme eventually failed, and he and his family left Medora in early 1887 (only four years after coming to the area). The marquis's lasting creation was Medora. The new and promising town quickly eclipsed Little Missouri and effectively shut down the little town on the west side of the river (the military cantonment had closed by early 1883).

Near the park entrance, Chimney Park State Historic Site contains the remnants of the Marquis de Mores's packing plant.

While Roosevelt and the marquis were in Medora, the little town experienced a huge boom. There was little in the way of law enforcement, and the town attracted a swarm of bad characters, including gunslingers, thieves, and murderers. As trains passed through town, the riffraff of Medora sometimes shot bullets into the train cars to frighten the passengers. The shady citizens of the town truly enjoyed enhancing Medora's reputation as a rough place. On at least one occasion, when a train stopped in Medora a group of misfits played a huge prank on the train's passengers. In a building in plain view of the train, the pranksters fired several gunshots and then hurried out the front door carrying a limp body. They circled around to the back of the building and then repeated the act. Their goal was to give train passengers the false impression that murder and mayhem were breaking loose in Medora.

The formation of the Little Missouri Stockmen's Association brought some law and order to Medora and the region, and the bad behavior that had made the community notorious became less frequent. After the departure of both Roosevelt and the marquis, Medora turned into a cattle town no more notable than any other in the West.

Modern Medora

Capitalizing on Medora's historical value, in 1958 a play about Roosevelt's life in the Badlands, *Old Four Eyes*, was put into production. Seven years later, the play was replaced by the Medora Musical. The musical has continued ever since and is one of the state's biggest tourist attractions. It takes place at the 2,900-seat Burning Hills Amphitheater, which even has a large outdoor escalator. Each night before the musical there is a Pitchfork Fondue, where juicy steaks are dipped by pitchfork into vats of hot oil. A friend of mine said the following about the Pitchfork Fondue: "It's worth it. It's quite fun to watch the employees grab a pitchfork from a huge arsenal, stick a large slab of beef on it, and thrust it into a large vat of oil. The quality of the beef itself was high. We were some of the younger folks there (most people were middle-aged or older), but everyone was friendly and having a ball. And it was great to eat outside in the fantastic late-summer weather of North Dakota."

In 2000 *Wooly Boys* was filmed in and around Medora. The movie stars Kris Kristofferson and Peter Fonda and at its heart is a tribute to the virtues of the simple North Dakota ranching lifestyle. In equally appropriate fashion, in 2005 the North Dakota Cowboy Hall of Fame opened its doors in Medora.

What Else Can I Do in Medora?

Not counting Theodore Roosevelt National Park, the Medora Musical and Pitchfork Fondue are Medora's primary attractions. They occur nightly from Memorial Day through Labor Day. The Pitchfork Fondue begins at 6:00 P.M., followed by the musical at 8:30 P.M. For more information or to buy tickets to these events, call (800) 633–6721 or visit www.medora.com.

There are numerous museums, historical sites, and educational programs in Medora. Just outside the park, the North Dakota Cowboy Hall of Fame is in an imposing building that is hard to miss. It has exhibits about North Dakota's cowboy history and about American Indians. For the TR enthusiast, an annual one-act play entitled *Bully* tells the story of Theodore Roosevelt. It occurs daily in summer. Check for times and locations. At De Mores State Historic Site you can visit the Marquis de Mores's twenty-six-room chateau. Nearby Chimney Park State Historic Site (free admission) provides a picnic area and protects the remnants of the marquis's packing plant. Site information is provided on interpretive panels.

The Harold Shafer Museum (free admission) tells the life story of an important North Dakota businessman and covers his career accomplishments and contributions to Medora. Shafer started the Gold Seal Company, which sold floor wax, then also glass wax, and later Snowy Bleach®, and Mr. Bubble®. He also started the Medora Musical.

The Doll House Museum allows visitors to see a collection of antique dolls and toys in a historic home. The Theodore Roosevelt National Park Visitor Center has exhibits about Roosevelt and the park. It is described more thoroughly in the next chapter. The Billings County Museum has artifacts and exhibits that cover the county's ranching history.

If you want to do some shopping, Medora has plenty of specialty shops and antiques-oriented stores. Two places of special interest are the Joe Ferris Store and Todd's Old Time Photo Parlor and Gift Shoppe. Roosevelt sometimes stayed in the building that his friend Joe Ferris operated, which today is a store that sells numerous items. At Todd's photo parlor you can have fun black-and-white photos made of yourself and friends in period dress with props.

For the golf enthusiast, the Bully Pulpit Golf Course is 3 miles south of town. It was ranked by *Golf Digest* as the country's best new and affordable public golf course in 2005. Call (800) 633–6721 or visit www.medora .com for rates. For the less serious golfer, there is minigolf in Medora as well. The town also has a public pool, tennis courts, and several children's playgrounds.

For those thirsting for a little bit of nightlife, the most consistent event is the Medora Musical. Otherwise, the Iron Horse Saloon and Restaurant usually has bands and dancing on the weekends. The Red Trail Campground offers nightly music; the Little Missouri Saloon also has music on occasion. The Badlands Pizza Parlor and Saloon is the other place that stays open late in Medora. If you like movies and don't mind a thirty-minute drive, the town of Belfield (to the east) has a historic movie theater that provides old-fashioned movie experiences. The Belfield Theatre (701–575–8140) is more than fifty years old and still regularly shows movies on weekends.

Where Can I Stay in Medora?

There are numerous camping and lodging options in and around Medora. Medora itself is in such a small geographical area that you should have little trouble finding the lodging options in Medora proper. Make sure you get good directions to the lodging options listed outside Medora, as it can be easy to get lost off the main roads. Other lodging possibilities are available in the small towns of Belfield and Beach. Belfield is 16 miles to the east of Medora; Beach is 23 miles west.

Camping

Buffalo Gap Campground (7 miles west of Medora on Interstate 94, exit 18). USDA Forest Service campground with primitive camping. Picnic table and fire ring with each site. Bathrooms with coin operated showers available. Open Memorial Day to Labor Day. (701) 225–5151; www.fs.fed.us/r1/dakotaprairie.

Medora Campground (West Pacific Avenue). Tent and RV camping; 124 sites with hookups, sewer for RVs available. Bathrooms, showers, laundry, and store. Open Memorial Day to Labor Day. (701) 623–4444 or (800) 633–6721; www.medora.com.

Red Trail Campground (250 East River Road South). Tent and RV camping; 100 sites with hookups, sewer for RVs available. Bathrooms, showers, and store. Free nightly entertainment. Open May through September. (701) 623–4317 or (800) 621–4317.

Sully Creek State Park (2.5 miles south of Medora; take East River Road South). Primitive camping for tents and RVs. Vault toilets and horse corrals. Open April through November. (701) 667–6340; www.ndparks.com.

Lodging

Motels and Hotels

AmericInn Motel and Suites (75 East River Road South). 56 rooms; AC, CATV, free continental breakfast, indoor pool w/sauna and Jacuzzi, laundry; pets allowed. Open year-round. (701) 623–4800 or (800) 634–3444; www.americinn.com.

Badlands Motel (501 Pacific Avenue). 115 rooms; AC, CATV, heated outdoor pool. Open April 15 through October 31. (701) 623–4444 or (800) 633–6721; www.medora.com.

The Bunkhouse (400 East River Road South). 160 rooms; AC, CATV, heated outdoor pool. Open Memorial Day through Labor Day. (701) 623–4444 or (800) 633–6721; www.medora.com.

Rough Riders Hotel (301 Third Avenue). 9 rooms; AC, CATV, restaurant. Hotel is a reconstruction in the location of a historic hotel where Theodore Roosevelt once stayed and gave a campaign speech. Open June through September. (701) 623–4444 or (800) 633–6721; www .medora.com.

B&Bs, Lodges, Ranches, and Cabins

Bar X Guest Ranch (9 miles south of Medora). Two cabins for rent on working ranch. Showers, hot tub; horseback riding available. (701) 623–4300.

Burkhardt House (near Medora Musical amphitheater). Space for up to ten people. Location is adjacent to the Medora Musical and Pitchfork Fondue. Open Memorial Day through Labor Day. (701) 623–4444 or (800) 633–6721; www.medora.com.

Buffalo Gap Guest Ranch and Trailhead (7 miles west of Medora, exit 18 off I–94). 10 rooms; bar and restaurant; horse accommodations, outfitting, shuttle, guide services, package deals available. Close to Maah Daah Hey and Buffalo Gap Trails. (701) 623–4200; www.buffalo gapguestranch.com; e-mail: buffalogapranch@midstate.net.

Camel's Hump Lodge (15 miles west of Medora, exit 10 off I–94). Lodge sleeps up to ten; 3 bedrooms, 1.5 bathrooms, full kitchen, dining room, TV, linens, gas grill; horse accommodations. 220 acres of private land available for recreation and hunting. Three-night minimum. (701) 575–4025; www.camelshumplodge.com.

Custer's Cottage (156 East River Road South). Two fully furnished apartments for rent in same house. Each has living room, private-entry access, AC, CATV, full kitchen, linens, laundry machines. One unit has 4 bedrooms, the other has 2. (701) 623–4378; www.custerscottage.com; e-mail: info@custerscottage.com.

Dakota Sky Ranch (far from Medora, between South and North Units of park). Cabin with 12 bunk beds, master bedroom, full kitchen and bath;

horse accommodations. Located near Maah Daah Hey Trail. (701) 565–2288.

Diamond Bar Bed and Breakfast (11 miles north of Medora, exit 23 off I–94). Primitive log cabin available for rent with modern facilities. Meals and entertainment are available (the storytellin' and guitar pickin' kind). (701) 623–4913; www.geocities.com/spin_a_yarn/page1.htm; e-mail: farmstro@westriv.com.

Eagle Ridge Lodge (7 miles west of Medora). 7 guest suites; meals, horse boarding, trail rides, and educational guide services available. Open all year and available for retreats and special events. (701) 623–2216; www.eagleridgelodge.com; e-mail: info@EagleRidgeLodge.com.

Little Missouri Bed and Corral (1 mile south of Medora). Fully furnished cabin with 2 bedrooms. Horse corrals available. Open April through November. (701) 623–4496; e-mail: owen@midstate.net.

Medora Cabins (near Medora Campground). Two cabins for rent, one large and one small. Each includes kitchenette, full bath, living room, bedroom, sleeping loft, and front porch. Small cabin sleeps up to six, large cabin up to eight. (701) 623–4444 or (800) 633–6721; www .medora.com.

T.R. Cabin & Ranch House (485 Sixth Street). T.R. Cabin is reproduction of Roosevelt's Maltese Cross ranch cabin and sleeps up to six. Ranch house is a separate building and also offers lodging. Open Memorial Day through Labor Day. (701) 623–4444 or (800) 633–6721; www .medora.com.

Wooly Boys Inn (Broadway). This unique lodging option has 2 bedrooms, a living room, a kitchenette, TV, and photographs from the film *Wooly Boys*. (800) 633–6721; www.woolyboysinn.com.

Belfield

Cowboy Inn (406 U.S. Highway 10 E). 21 rooms; AC, CATV. (701) 575–4245.

Trapper's Inn (Junction I–94 and U.S. Highway 85). 70 rooms; AC, CATV, refrigerator, restaurant, heated pool. (701) 575–4261 or (800) 284–1855.

Beach

Buckboard Inn (1191 First Avenue NW). 39 rooms; AC, CATV, continental breakfast, pets allowed. (701) 872–4794.

The Outpost (3291 Highway 16). 15 rooms; AC, CATV. (701) 872–4717.
WestGate Badlands Motel 10 rooms; AC, CATV. (701) 872–4521.

Where Can I Get Food in Medora?

Medora has numerous food options during summer. At other times of the year, while you will still be able to find a place to eat, you might not have many options. For steaks, burgers, soups, salads, and sandwiches, restaurants include the Bully Cafe, Chuckwagon Buffet, Cowboy Cafe, Iron Horse Saloon and Restaurant, Little Missouri Dining Room and Saloon, Maltese Burgers, and Roughrider Hotel Dining Room. The Badlands Pizza Parlor and Saloon, as you can guess, is your best option for pizza. All of these restaurants are within a short walk of one another. For more than your standard cup of coffee, try either James Gang Java or Hidden Springs Java. There are also numerous ice-cream stores and a few other places to grab snacks and sandwiches. The Pitchfork Fondue (see the "What Can I Do in Medora?" section) is also an option for dinner.

Other Services

A post office is located on Third Avenue, as well as an ATM at the First State Bank. ATMs can also be found at other locations in Medora. The only place to get gasoline is the Medora Service Station on Pacific Avenue. The Billings County Resource Center and Library (on Broadway) offers Internet access for $1.00 and has wireless access at the same cost. It is not open on Saturday or Sunday, and the hours vary by season. There are three churches in town: Catholic, First Congregational, and Lutheran.

Outfitters

The Buffalo Gap Guest Ranch listed earlier offers outfitting and guide services, as does Elkhorn Outfitters (701–565–2310). Guided bike trips are led by Dakota Cyclery Mountain Bike Adventures (see the Other Recreation Possibilities chapter). Horseback riding trips are offered by the Peaceful Valley Ranch and the Medora Riding Stables (see the Walk Softly and Carry a Big Stick chapter).

Touring the South Unit: Dog Towns, Painted Canyons, and Petrified Forests

When you are making your way through the South Unit of Theodore Roosevelt National Park, you might feel like you are revisiting the scenery and sets of the movie *Dances with Wolves*. While the movie was not filmed here, the park preserves an ecosystem similar to the western prairies that were shown in the film and can definitely create the same inspirational feeling. Prairie dog towns are one of the fundamental ecosystem features here. Today we call this type of habitat grasslands, or mixed grass prairie. The buttes and other geological features of the South Unit badlands add interest to the mixed-grass prairie you see here.

In the South Unit you can also enjoy forested slopes and draws, cottonwood stands, small creeks, and the banks of the Little Missouri River. If you have the time and interest, then you should definitely take advantage of the less-traveled areas and less-common recreational opportunities. For example, if the water level is high enough, you might enjoy a summer float down the Little Missouri River by canoe. You could also bike the South Unit's loop road—but these are just a couple ideas. There are countless sight-seeing and recreational possibilities in the South Unit of the park. I hope you seize the opportunity to experience some of them.

The Visitor Center Area

After passing through the park entrance and paying the entry fee, it is a good idea to spend some time in the visitor center. Here you can get information from knowledgeable park staff members, view interesting exhibits (including one of a unique dinosaur skeleton), see a thirteen-minute park film, get backcountry camping permits, check for a schedule of the summer's interpretive programs, purchase books at the Theodore Roosevelt Nature & History Association bookstore, and, most importantly, tour Theodore Roosevelt's Maltese Cross Cabin.

In the summer season (June through September), park interpreters provide guided tours through Roosevelt's Maltese Cross Cabin and explain his legacy in the West. At other times of year you can walk through the cabin on your own and view its furnishings through Plexiglas. Some of the items in the cabin belonged to Roosevelt, such as the writing desk and a large storage trunk. At this desk he wrote one of his many books, *Hunting Trips of a Ranchman*. The cabin itself has an interesting history. It was moved several times for people to see in places as far away as Portland, Oregon, and St. Louis, Missouri. It was eventually moved here (several miles from its original location), as the park seemed like an appropriate place for it to be.

Once you begin driving on the park's scenic loop drive, use caution and watch for wildlife on or near the road. A brief stop just up the road at the Medora Overlook will give you a vista of the small community below. After the overlook, in about 2 miles you will drive over a bridge that crosses Interstate 94 and leads you to Johnson Plateau.

Johnson Plateau

As you drove down I–94 to get to the park, you might have noticed that a 7-foot-high fence encloses the park. Perhaps you also noticed this after taking the bridge across I–94 that leads to Johnson Plateau. Why is the park fenced? It all comes down to a simple matter of keeping some of the park's larger animals from getting outside the park. Once you arrive at Johnson Plateau, you might see some of these giants in the prairie dog town here—foraging or lounging only a short distance from the road. What are these magnificent animals?

Excuse Me, Sir, but Is It Buffalo or Bison?

While both terms can be used to refer to these charismatic animals, bison is the scientifically correct term. The use of the name "buffalo" evolved from a French word for cattle: les boeufs. Putting names aside, bison are amazing creatures. They are the largest North American land mammals, and males can weigh more than 2,000 pounds. The power of these wild animals should not be questioned, and you should not approach them (stay at least 100 yards away when possible). And there is a lot more to know about bison.

Hunted nearly to extinction in the late 1800s, thanks to conservation efforts bison have made a comeback in the park.

Before telling the story of this animal's journey from being a near historical memory to being perhaps the enduring symbol of the American West, here's a little more about the characteristics and behavior of bison.

Bison generally form large herds in the summer months, and these herds remain together until fall. This time is the mating season, also known as the "rut." Competition among males (known as bulls) for females (known as cows) can be intense but interesting to watch—from a safe distance. The herds can also be quite noisy. Grunts and snorts can often be heard from miles away. After the rut, most of the young bulls disperse into small groups, and the older bulls generally roam as individuals. Cows and yearlings stay together throughout the year. Calves

continued

are born in early spring, and these youngsters often display much more frisky behavior than the adults, running about playfully, sometimes chasing one another. A bison's fur grows long for the winter months and sheds to a lighter layer for summer. Its diet consists of grass. In wintertime a bison will use its huge head and horns to plow into the snow in search of any grass that remains below. They can survive in extremely low temperatures. The general life expectancy for bison ranges from about ten to twelve years—although some individuals have lived thirty to forty years.

The size of the South Unit's herd varies from year to year and usually ranges from 250 to 450 animals. The North Unit's herd generally has 100 to 300 animals. Periodically the park holds a roundup to "cull" the herd. Nonprofit groups apply for the culled bison, and many are sold to the Three Affiliated Tribes of North Dakota. The park's managers take out bison periodically to make sure the park's habitat can adequately support a healthy number of bison.

It is believed that there were once about sixty million bison in North America. The Mandan, Hidatsa, Arikara (now known as the Three Affiliated Tribes), Lakota, and other native peoples hunted bison but in most cases took animals in moderation. They used many or all of the parts of a bison for food, medicine, and other practical purposes. On some occasions, native peoples created bison stampedes over "buffalo jumps"—large cliffs or overhangs—to enable easier and safer killing of bison. This method of hunting was also sometimes wasteful. The magnitude of the waste, however, did not match that of the settlers who came later.

In the 1830s hunters and settlers began shooting bison on a massive scale. Bison hides sold for a high price, and bison tongues were considered a delicacy. Their bones were collected and sold as fertilizer. All of this killing led to the near extinction of bison—and to the end of many native peoples' way of life, as bison was their primary food source.

Theodore Roosevelt fulfilled a dualistic role of hunter and savior when it came to bison. In fact, he first came to the Little Missouri River Badlands to shoot a bison. After a ten-day guided search, he succeeded in shooting and killing a modest-size bull. As legend goes, he then hollered in delight and ran around the fallen giant. But as the reality of their decimation became apparent, Roosevelt realized that the indiscriminate killing of bison needed to stop. With some luck and the help of conservationists like Roosevelt, a few hundred bison survived—the breeding stock for all bison we have in the United States today. The story of the bison's plight and recovery might be viewed as both a cautionary and an inspirational tale of the impact we humans can have upon the world we live in—for better and for worse.

To learn more about Roosevelt's experience in the badlands, take a short tour of his Maltese Cross Cabin, located at the South Unit Visitor Center.

If you do not see bison on Johnson Plateau, do not fret—you will probably see them later.

But there is good news! While on Johnson Plateau it is almost impossible not to see prairie dogs. Prairie dog towns are unique places that provide a window for viewing nature's vivid web of life. Johnson Plateau offers you the first of several chances to observe what goes on in a prairie dog town, and usually a patient visit is rewarded.

You are also welcome to walk through prairie dog towns, but understand that if an animal has to act in a nonhabitual way because of you, then you are probably having too much of an effect on that animal's behavior. Resist the temptation to get too close to prairie dogs or feed them—they bite, and your food might make them sick. Prairie dog towns are also the homes to prairie rattlesnakes—the park's only venomous snake species—so watch your step. Black widow spiders sometimes choose to live in prairie dog burrows and will make their presence felt with a painful bite. Keep your eyes out for both of these creatures, and do not let young children wander through a prairie dog town alone or stick their hands into prairie dog burrows. That being said, all wild creatures should be respected, not feared. All play important roles in the ecosystem you see here. While these precautions and dangers are important to know about, don't let them scare you from taking a little trip into a prairie dog town.

After your visit to the prairie dog town, a short drive will bring you to the Skyline Vista Trail. This 0.2-mile round-trip wheelchair-accessible trail provides an excellent opportunity for viewing the North Dakota landscapes that lie beyond the park.

Who was Johnson Plateau named for? T. E. Johnson was a homesteader and rancher who lived in this area before it was a park. Many places in the park are named for people who homesteaded or ranched in the park area at one time or another.

After leaving the Johnson Plateau area, you will be headed down toward Cottonwood Campground. You will get your first views of the Little Missouri River from inside the park on this short descent. Stop for a moment to check out the interpretive sign at the River Woodland Overlook, just beyond Mile Marker 5 on your left.

Cottonwood Campground

Descending into the valley below Johnson Plateau, you will find Cottonwood Campground, a beautiful place that offers easy access to the Little Missouri River. For those who are not camping, there is a nice picnic area for your use. If you're camping, here are the essentials:

- The campground has 76 sites and does not offer reservations.
- One family group or six persons and two vehicles are allowed to camp at any one campsite.
- A group site is available for 6 to 20 persons. Reservations are accepted.
- The campground offers flush toilets and running water during the summer months; each site has a picnic table and grill. There are no showers or other amenities.
- There are many pull-through sites for trailers and RVs but no hookups or dump stations. Generator hours are 8:00 A.M. to 8:00 P.M.

Are Prairie Dogs Really Dogs?

Early French explorers called prairie dogs *petit chiens* (little dogs) because of the piercing alarm call they make to warn other prairie dogs of danger's presence. There are five species of prairie dogs in the United States. The ones you see here are black-tailed prairie dogs. While they are rodents and not actually dogs, prairie dogs do share at least one trait with our canine friends—they are some of the most vigilant creatures you will ever see.

Many animals consider prairie dogs to be a good meal. For this reason, prairie dogs chop down all the tall grasses around their communal living areas, known as "towns," and spend a lot of their day barking and watching the sky and horizon. They have different barks for ground predators like coyotes and aerial predators like golden eagles. When an alarm bark is heard, a prairie dog will run toward the nearest escape hole, or burrow. It will then also begin to bark on top of the "watch-tower" mound that it has made on top of the burrow and continue until a threat is gone. A prairie dog can also escape by running into a burrow. Some burrows in prairie dog towns are interconnected by underground tunnels.

Although protected in the park, prairie dog populations are decreasing nationwide.

Prairie dogs are fun to watch. They have a complex system of communication and will often interact with one another in humorous ways. For instance, prairie dogs are well known for jumping and making a simultaneous "yip" sound. This "jump-yip" call is probably a territorial signal. Be on the lookout for this interesting behavior.

In addition to serving as food for other animals, prairie dogs have a positive influence on the ecosystem around them. Their burrows provide homes for other animals, and their eating patterns encourage the growth of a wide diversity of plant species. Prairie dogs eat grasses and flowering plants (sometimes known as forbs). They seem to know when to eat what, since plant diversity is generally in balance. The wide array of short plants attracts insects and other small animals like rabbits. In turn, this migration attracts predators like burrowing owls (which chase insects on the ground) and prairie rattlesnakes (which enjoy rodents and rabbits). A few lucky animals sometimes are able to work close to home. For instance, badgers often live and hunt in prairie dog towns.

continued

Bison are also often found in prairie dog towns, as these areas provide enough soil for bison to "wallow" (roll back and forth on their sides). Nobody understands exactly why bison wallow. Some people have speculated that it is part of a mating ritual. Others believe that bison think it is fun and that maybe it helps soothe the itches of their summer coats or helps eliminate parasites. Bison also like the grass in or near prairie dog towns. As the grass in prairie dog towns must grow quickly and efficiently before being eaten by prairie dogs, it probably has more nutritional content per bite, making it an attractive food for bison.

Despite the key role prairie dogs play in this type of ecosystem, they are not loved by all. Human needs for ranching and farmland have taken much of their habitat. Ranchers often poison or shoot prairie dogs, viewing them as pests. As a result, one of their most important predators is now one of the most endangered animals in the United States. The black-footed ferret was thought to be extinct until a small group was found in Wyoming in 1981. They almost exclusively eat prairie dogs and did not fare well as prairie dog populations declined across the West. Recovery efforts to reintroduce black-footed ferrets to some of their historic ranges are now occurring.

But the issue of the black-footed ferret's decline gets back to why ranchers tend not to like prairie dogs. Many ranchers believe that prairie dogs will decrease their profits by eating grass their cattle need. If your livelihood depended on having as much range as possible for your livestock, do you think you would be a friend to the prairie dog?

This brings us to perhaps the most important question about prairie dogs: Is it possible to be both a rancher and a conservationist? More and more people think so. Coexistence is the key to most successful conservation efforts in the United States today. With a little effort, we can usually allow for both the preservation of nature and the needs of people. Prairie dogs can survive. They, like bison, symbolize a part of the United States' past that is worth remembering, and hopefully they will have places to live in and outside our parks in the future.

A badger eyes a vigilant prairie dog at Johnson Plateau.

People aren't the only animals who appreciate the tall cottonwood trees, nearby river, and relaxing environs of Cottonwood Campground.

- The campground is open year-round and may fill on summer weekends.
- In the summer months, park staff members present interpretive campfire programs at the campground amphitheater.
- Pets are allowed but must be on a leash less than 6 feet long. Pets cannot be left unattended or allowed to approach wildlife.

Approximately 1 mile after passing Cottonwood Campground, you will reach the point where the actual "loop" portion of the South Unit road begins. Regardless of which direction you choose, you will eventually end up in the same place. Most people choose to go straight and do the loop in a counterclockwise fashion. The order in which I discuss the South Unit is also organized in this order. A *Roadlog Guide* is available for the park. If using that guide, it is important to follow the mile markers in this direction.

Plant Communities in the Park

If you are interested in plants and wildflowers and want a guide, I recommend *Wildflowers, Grasses & Other Plants of the Northern Plains and Black Hills* by Theodore Van Bruggen. It is sold at all the park's visitor centers. The mixed-grass prairie ecosystems that you will find in Theodore Roosevelt National Park have become a rarity in the United States. The park boasts more than 400 plant species within its borders—a tribute to the protection it provides. Seventeen species of grasses grow in the park, although four of these are exotic (nonnative) species. But while there is a lot of diversity in grass, you will not see as much diversity when it comes to trees in the park. The dominant tree here is Rocky Mountain juniper, easily seen throughout the park on the north-facing slopes of buttes. Near the Little Missouri River, creeks, and other moist areas, you will also see cottonwood, green ash, box elder, and American elm. As for shrubs, make sure that you take a moment and rub your fingers over one of the varieties of sagebrush in the park. Notice the pleasant smell you will have on your fingers. But all is not well among the plants here in the park. Exotic plant species have become a major problem and are discussed later in this chapter.

The Burning Coal Vein/Buck Hill Area

The Burning Coal Vein/Buck Hill area of the park contains some fascinating places where you will want to stop. As you continue past the loop road junction, you will first drive through another prairie dog town. Several miles down the road you will reach the Scoria Point Overlook. At this semi-circle pullout you will get another view into the vastness of the Badlands. As the overlook's name suggests, here you can see red-colored rocks that are known locally as "scoria" or "clinker." Actually these rocks are porcelanite. They usually have a brick-red color, making them very distinctive. You can see clinker in many places throughout the park. It is a sediment that has been baked by a burning coal seam. True scoria is actually volcanic in origin and is not found in the park.

In 1.5 miles you will come to the Ridgeline Trail. This self-guided interpretive nature trail is a 0.8-mile loop. A brief uphill segment occurs at the beginning of the trail and several other times throughout its route. The North Dakota Badlands Overlook is just a bit farther down the road and offers another view of the badlands from a semicircle parking area similar to the one at Scoria Point.

The park's Old East Entrance can be seen by taking a short 0.4-mile hike from the pullout just before Mile Marker 13 (about 1.5 miles beyond the North Dakota Badlands Overlook). Until 1967 a road leading past this historic structure allowed visitors to enter the park from the Painted Canyon area. See the Walk Softly and Carry a Big Stick chapter for more information about the Old East Entrance hike.

You will next pass a junction for the Lower and Upper Paddock Creek Trails. The Lower Paddock Creek Trail ends at the opposite end of the scenic loop drive. The Upper Paddock Creek Trail goes to the eastern boundary of the South Unit. Parking is available slightly farther down the road. These trails are discussed more in this chapter and in the Walk Softly and Carry a Big Stick chapter.

From here it is about a 1-mile journey to a short dirt road on your right that leads to the self-guided Coal Vein Trail. This interesting 0.8-mile loop trail offers the story of a coal vein that burned here continuously from 1951 until 1977. An interpretive sign and a self-guiding brochure help tell the story as you walk the trail.

Once back on the main loop road, it is about 1.5 miles to the road that leads to Buck Hill. Take this right turn and travel 1 mile up to the Buck Hill parking area. At 2,855 feet, Buck Hill is the second highest point in the South Unit and the park. Peck Hill, located near Painted Canyon, is 2,865 feet—just 10 feet higher. A somewhat steep 0.1-mile trail leads up from the circular parking area to a ridge and provides you with a 360-degree view of the South Unit. Buck Hill was most likely named for the numerous deer that live in the park. In addition to the two species of deer (mule and white-tailed) that live in the South Unit, there is also a healthy population of elk.

Half a mile after Buck Hill you will see where the Talkington Trail crosses the loop road. This 8.1-mile trail is named for a family that once owned the land in this area of the park and traverses a large portion of the South Unit, starting from the east boundary and finishing near the north boundary. The trail distance is almost perfectly bisected by the road (to the east from here it is 4.0 miles; to the north it is 4.1 miles). Continuing onward you will be headed through the northern areas of the South Unit on your way to the Wind Canyon area.

Elk: A New Management Challenge

In 1985 a small herd of elk was reintroduced to the park. Historically elk had lived in North Dakota but became extinct here because of overharvesting. As part of a larger and functioning ecosystem, elk belong here. You can easily recognize them—they look different from the deer in the park. They are much larger and have a distinctive section of white or tan fur on their rumps (look for the contrast in color from the majority of their bodies). Listen for the majestic and exotic-sounding "bugles" of the bulls (males) during the fall mating season.

The bad news is that now the park is dealing with a serious elk problem. There are too many! Even though elk can move freely in and out of the park's boundaries, they choose to stay in the park more often than leaving. Without any effective natural predators in the park, the elk population in the South Unit now exceeds 700 animals—probably more than the park's grazing resources can handle.

At the time of this writing, the park cannot meet its population objectives for elk because it does not have an approved plan for managing the animals. Mike Oehler, the park's wildlife biologist, explains that "right now with the increasing elk population, there's no way to reduce the population because of the disease concerns that have tied our hands. In the past we used to round up elk and then give them to other state or federal agencies involved in elk restoration programs."

The disease concerns Oehler talks about relate to chronic wasting disease, or CWD, a contagious neurological disease that affects deer and elk. It causes deer and elk to gradually lose weight and start showing other symptoms, eventually leading to the animal's death. The National Park Service only permits animals to be moved from park areas if the populations they are part of are statistically free of the disease. Currently all available methods to test elk for CWD are lethal, since an animal's brain must be examined to confirm the disease. Researchers continue to look for a way to test live elk for the disease.

Although no animals have yet tested positive for CWD in North Dakota, Theodore Roosevelt National Park can do little about its growing elk population. The park is currently working on an Elk Management Plan and an Environmental Impact Statement that will lay the groundwork for elk management. Oehler is optimistic about finding a solution and reasons that "what we do with one species has the potential to affect other species. If we look at reducing elk numbers because of overgrazing, we certainly want to consider other options as well. For instance, maybe we can do things with bison populations or wild horse populations until a management plan for elk is in place."

The Wind Canyon Area

About 3 miles beyond the Buck Hill road, you will find a series of three pullouts that are known as the Boicourt Overlook. The overlook is named for the Boicourt family, who once had a homestead a few miles from this area. Looking to the south from the overlooks, you see thickly vegetated north-facing slopes. Looking to the north from the overlooks, you get a quick reality check as you view the encroaching oil rigs that are located outside the park.

Down the road about 0.5 mile later, while going downhill look for a large piece of petrified wood in the flat area to your right. Just a short distance beyond, you will pass a parking area on your left that is one of the trailheads for the Jones Creek Trail. Jones Creek was probably named for "Hell-Roarin'" Bill Jones: a colorful Medora resident who at times got into trouble. The 3.6-trail parallels a creek and eventually links to another portion of the loop road, intersecting the Talkington Trail along the way.

For the next 4 miles you will be skirting the South Unit's northern boundaries as you travel. Eventually you will reach an intersection where you can turn either left or right. A dirt road to the right leads to the north boundary of the South Unit and the Roundup Horse Camp. The Roundup Horse Camp can be reserved by groups that plan on bringing horses to the park, or by any large group for that matter. More information about the Roundup area is available in the Walk Softly and Carry a Big Stick chapter. The road is also one of the routes for traveling to the Elkhorn Ranch. You should definitely check with park staff for road and river conditions before making this trip.

To continue back toward the park entrance, turn left at the intersection and continue for about 0.5 mile to the Wind Canyon parking area, on your right. Wind Canyon is a place where you can see geological forces in action. The Wind Canyon Trail has an interpretive sign that discusses the interesting wind- and water-made sandstone shapes you will see here. There is also a fantastic view of the Little Missouri River bending below as it heads north toward the South Unit's boundary. The trail is 0.5-mile round-trip. After leaving the Wind Canyon area, you will be heading toward the Peaceful Valley Area. Before we discuss what you can see and do there, it is a good opportunity (see sidebar) to discuss predators found in the park—this area is an excellent place to be watching for coyotes.

It's Good to Be the King: Predators in the Park

To slightly alter an old joke I once heard in a VFW bingo parlor: "Some days it's so hot in Theodore Roosevelt National Park that you can see coyotes chasing prairie dogs . . . and they're walking!" Hopefully the knee slapping that is now ensuing hasn't hurt you too much, but coyotes walking after prairie dogs is something I have actually seen in the park. Usually you'll see a coyote bursting into a prairie dog town at full sprint, using the element of surprise as it attempts to grab a fast meal. Sometimes their hunts are unsuccessful, and they will then meander through a prairie dog town, perhaps hoping for some unsuspecting prairie dog to let down its guard. Coyotes are sometimes known to partner with badgers, another predator that lives in the park. Coyotes will stand near one prairie dog burrow, while badgers dig into a burrow hole thought to connect to the other hole the coyote is watching. Needless to say, this is not a good situation for a prairie dog trapped inside. Badgers are easy to identify—their strange digging-oriented body is framed by a distinctive black and white–striped face. These black-and-white markings serve as a warning to other animals that badgers are not to be messed with. In addition to coyotes and badgers, there are many other types of predators in the park, including bull snakes, burrowing owls, great horned owls, robber flies, dragonflies, mountain lions, bobcats, golden eagles, northern harriers, and spade-footed toads.

Predators play important roles in ecosystems by helping to regulate the populations of other animals, particularly herbivores—animals that eat plants. Coyotes are the predator kings of this park. They often take prairie dogs, deer fawns, rabbits, and insects. They scavenge carcasses when they are available. Visitors often think that they see wolves in the park, but remember that to many native peoples, the coyote is known as "the Trickster." While there are no wolves here today, there are some really large coyotes. Grizzly bears were here in TR's time but today are no longer found in the North Dakota badlands. Mountain lions (also known as cougars, pumas, and catamounts) do sometimes make their way into the park, hunting deer as their primary prey. You would be extremely lucky to see one. Enjoy any sightings of coyotes or other predators here, as it's a chance to see some of nature's hunters at work in the wild.

The Peaceful Valley Area

Driving down the hill from Wind Canyon, you will again travel through prairie dog towns and will eventually reach the Beef Corral Bottom Pullout. An interpretive sign here explains how this was probably the location of one of the Marquis de Mores's cattle corrals (the marquis was the founder of Medora). A mile farther down the road you will find the other trailhead for the Jones Creek Trail on your left. Here an interpretive sign informs visitors about the Civilian Conservation Corps (CCC) and the role they played in the park. At one time there was a CCC camp right across the road from the Jones Creek parking area, although it is not obvious.

Look for an unpaved road on the left after journeying a mile farther. This short road leads to the other end of the Lower Paddock Creek Trail and a prairie dog town—one of my favorite areas in the park. The 4.4-mile Lower Paddock Creek Trail first takes you through the prairie dog town and continues on through the Badlands, paralleling Paddock Creek most of the way and taking you through several more prairie dog towns. The trail allows you to explore lesser used wildlife trails and see some of the interior of the South Unit. The creek was named for one of Medora's most intriguing bad guys, E. G. Paddock, who at one time had a cabin near the creek.

Shortly after the road to the Lower Paddock Creek Trail, look for the Peaceful Valley Ranch on your right. This is a good place to keep your eyes open for people riding horses near the road. A park concessionaire offers guided horseback tours, starting from the ranch. More information about going on a horseback riding tour with the folks at Peaceful Valley Ranch is included in the Walk Softly and Carry a Big Stick chapter. If you have seen the park's wild horses, see the accompanying sidebar for more information about them.

A short distance after you pass the Peaceful Valley Ranch, you will return to the scenic loop road junction. Turn right and you will be headed back out of the park on the stretch of road you have already traveled. See if you notice anything different this time.

The Painted Canyon Area

The only stop many people make at Theodore Roosevelt National Park is at the Painted Canyon Visitor Center. It is a short detour off I–94. The visitor center building is generally open early April through mid-November, but you can stop here at any time of year and walk to the overlook. The vis-

The view from the Painted Canyon Visitor Center is a favorite with visitors.

itor center offers restrooms, exhibits about the park, and a bookstore run by the Theodore Roosevelt Nature & History Association. Sometimes bison hang out in or near the parking lot—to the delight of both casual and serious park visitors.

From behind the visitor center you can see the beautiful, varied colors of Painted Canyon and see Buck and Peck Hills in the distance. Several interpretive signs here tell about the canyon and the park. For a short hike take the steep 0.9-mile Painted Canyon Nature Trail loop that starts near the picnic shelter. This trail has a good diversity of plants and wildflowers. The 2.0-mile Painted Canyon Trail provides a connection for reaching the Upper Paddock Creek Trail. This is not a trail I recommend for casual hiking; it is extremely steep.

As you drive east of the Painted Canyon area, the flats you can see within the park fence are a good place to look for pronghorn, the fastest animals in North America. While figures vary, pronghorn can reach speeds of 50 miles per hour or higher. To distinguish them from deer, look for their white underbellies, forked horns, slim bodies, and inquisitive behavior.

The Petrified Forest

The Petrified Forest is located in the western wilderness area of the South Unit. Using even the shortest of routes, a hike of some distance is required

The Wild Horses of the American West

Horses first came to North America in the sixteenth century with the Spanish. As small numbers of horses escaped here and there from human containment, they began to form small bands that eventually became large bands of feral (wild) horses. (Feral animals are once-domesticated animals that have become wild.) Horses can be credited with changing Native Americans' way of life by offering a new method of transportation and hunting. Wild horses became part of the story of the American West and for some time roamed in great numbers, until a campaign to rid the West of "nuisance" horses began. A small herd of about 60 to 140 horses lives within the protection of Theodore Roosevelt National Park today. On occasion the horses are rounded up and some individuals removed to help keep a sustainable habitat for those that will remain in the South Unit of the park.

to get to the Petrified Forest (at least 3.0 miles round-trip). More than 20 miles of trails can be used to access the forest, a place where few living trees are actually standing today. The name is a little deceiving. Petrified wood is often seen in small pieces and is the product of a geological process where ancient wood has turned to stone. (*NOTE:* It is illegal to collect petrified wood in the park.) If you have the time and initiative to make a journey into the Petrified Forest, it is likely that you will walk out with a smile on your face. You will probably see few other people if you go.

This stump of petrified wood lies along the loop road.

The easiest way to reach the Petrified Forest is by driving around the western boundary of the park. Before heading to the Petrified Forest, ask park staff for directions and current information about trail and road conditions.

The Role of Fire in the Park

If you ever pay attention to the news, you have probably heard a lot recently about large "out-of-control wildfires" that seem to be burning around the nation almost every year. The truth is that you are only getting a part of the story. While wildfires can and do destroy people's homes and property—even lives—they can also be beneficial to ecosystems. Smokey Bear himself has recently amended his message to incorporate the positive aspects of fire in ecosystems.

So do wildfires occur in Theodore Roosevelt National Park? Yes. Beth Card, who recently served as the National Park Service's fire management officer in North Dakota, explains that "historically there have been wildfires and human-caused fires in the area. These intentional fires were set to help with hunting, for habitat control, and for warfare."

In 2000 the park experienced a large wildfire. Known as the "Painted Canyon Fire," the fire began with a lightning strike and burned in Painted Canyon. About 288 acres of land burned, including many trees and areas of grass. In fact, numerous species of grasses in the park provide the main "fuel" that burns in the badlands. According to Card, a grass fire "moves fast but goes out fast." Likewise, grass that burns recovers much faster than trees do. For this reason, evidence of burning in a place like Painted Canyon is hard to find several years after a fire.

Animals return quickly to burn areas, as fires encourage a diverse array of plants to grow. Card notes that new plant shoots in burn areas are sometimes referred to as "elk candy," since the shoots are "like candy to animals." Fires can also help get rid of plants that have established monocultures (areas with only one plant species). They also encourage native plant growth and can help to eliminate unwanted exotic plants.

Along with a history of fires in the North Dakota badlands area is a history of suppressing them. While Theodore Roosevelt lived in the area, he helped to suppress a fire on at least one occasion. Beth Card notes that fire suppression over the past 150 years has "made a major impact upon the landscape." What she means is that native plant communities have been eclipsed in many places by exotic species and plant monocultures. As fire plays an important role in habitat enhancement, a major component of Card's job has been to help restore the role of fire to the ecosystems of North Dakota's National Park Service sites. In addition to fighting fires, Card and other fire personnel also sometimes initiate what are known as prescribed burns (after a lot of planning and paperwork, that is). These burns aim to restore fire in a manner that is safe while meeting the goal of using fire as a positive tool for improving habitat and vegetation quality.

Hopefully more and more people will learn to recognize fire not only for its potentially devastating effects on people's lives but also for its positive effects on the health of habitats in places like Theodore Roosevelt National Park.

The War against Exotic Plants

One of the big ecological problems in Theodore Roosevelt National Park and the rest of the American West today is that exotic plant species are out-competing native species for living space. In other words, invasive plants are taking habitat away from the species that have traditionally occupied North Dakota and other western states. While some people might argue that this process is just nature taking its course, many of these plants have traveled great distances and arrived because of humans. Some of these species do not simply blend into the ecosystem's mosaic but can eventually dominate an ecosystem or even establish themselves as monocultures. They can take over because the native animals and environmental controls in habitats are often not adequate to control the population growth of exotic plants. These plants are destroying ecosystems and are also taking away usable land from farmers and ranchers.

The park is home base for a team of people who work exclusively on controlling exotic plant species with an arsenal of biological, chemical, and mechanical methods of control. They are the Northern Great Plains Exotic Plant Management Team. Taryn Flesjer, a biologist for the team, says that in Theodore Roosevelt National Park, "we concentrate on the rivers, streams, and trails because that's where the weeds (i.e., exotic plants) tend to congregate the most. They like water."

While there are many exotic plants on the verge of making their way into the park, leafy spurge and Canada thistle are the primary exotic plant species the park currently attempts to control. To identify leafy spurge, start by looking for a plant with a clump of small yellow flowers at the top of a green stalk. If you see lots of these plants together, chances are that they are leafy spurge. Spurge roots can extend more than 15 feet underground. No animals in the park eat spurge because it produces a milky latex that can irritate the skin. Leafy spurge is extremely hard to eliminate. The park sprays spurge by foot and by helicopter, but the most effective control the park uses is flea beetles, which are released to feed on spurge.

Canada thistle is another of the park's pernicious invaders. Despite its name, the plant is not from Canada. It has become associated with our friendly northern neighbor for a more sinister reason: its current reign of terror there. To identify Canada thistle, look for a plant with a pretty purple flower atop a spiny stalk. Despite its pleasant appearance, thistle is an enemy in the park. It establishes itself quickly, and its spiny stalks discourage most animals from eating it. To control thistle, the park sprays it.

While leafy spurge and Canada thistle are the main culprits in the park, other exotic species, like knapweed, are knocking on the door and are threatening to enter the park. One of the most serious of these threats is a tree called tamarisk, or salt cedar. According to Flesjer, "One adult tamarisk can use 200 gallons of water per day. So in an area that's arid like the park, we want to find it and stop it." Tamarisk has already been found in all three sections of the park.

What can you do to help stop the spread of exotic plants? Taryn Flesjer says that the park always appreciates reports from visitors about the location of exotic plants such as tamarisk. She also suggests that "wherever you go in the park, there's going to be some exotic plants. So it's beneficial if you can wash your gear before you enter the park and then after you leave to prevent the spread of plants to other places."

Touring the North Unit: Cannonballs, an Oxbow, and Solitude

While the North Unit of Theodore Roosevelt National Park is a less-visited area, it is not without its charms. Here you can still see the curious beauty of the Little Missouri River Badlands, watch for a wide variety of wildlife, and enjoy numerous recreation opportunities. A 14-mile drive-in, drive-out road provides access to the unit.

You will often read that when visiting the North Unit there is a strong possibility that you will not see any other people. You might also read that the North Unit is where you will get some of the premier (or best) views in the park. While I think these observations have some value, I also believe that they do not fully describe how the North Unit is different from—and also similar to—the South Unit. Let's talk about the observation that you are more likely to find solitude here than at the South Unit first.

At 24,070 acres, the North Unit is a little more than half the size of the South Unit (46,159 acres). Because it is smaller, it attracts less attention. More importantly, it is not on the interstate or a major highway, making it a detour for many travelers. It does not have a gateway community right at its front door (Watford City is 15 miles north). Instead of a loop road like the South Unit, it has the drive-in, drive-out road. To see a prairie dog town in the North Unit, you have to hike about a mile into the backcountry. Why *wouldn't* the South Unit be more popular with its larger size, easier access, gateway community, loop road, and more-accessible prairie dog towns? But while it's true that fewer people go to the North Unit, remember that the park as a whole does not get a very large number of visitors. Almost every place in the park has great potential to provide visitors with moments of solitude. In my experience, you are equally likely to not see many (or any!) other people while driving the road or exploring the South Unit's back-country.

As for the observation that the North Unit has some fantastic views, I think that this statement has some merit. But beauty is in the eye of the beholder, is it not? From a practical standpoint, what you get in the North Unit are more views of the Little Missouri River from higher vantage points at places like the River Bend and Oxbow Overlooks. These vistas and others allow you to see the Little Missouri curving through the badlands—something that is harder to see from the road in the South Unit.

Todd Stoeberl, the North Unit's district naturalist, describes the North Unit as being "a lot more rugged" than the South Unit. He also notes that "one main difference most people do not realize is that over half of the North Unit is designated as wilderness." What this means is that many of the hiking trails and views you get in the North Unit are in areas that have received the highest level of protection that the United States government provides to its public lands.

One last thing to note about the North Unit is that there are some differences in the wildlife you can see in comparison to the South Unit. This unit has no elk and or wild horses. On the other hand, you do have a chance to see bighorn sheep here, as well as a historic demonstration herd of long-horn cattle—two species that you cannot see in the South Unit. As previously mentioned, you must hike to see a prairie dog town when visiting the North Unit.

All in all, the North and South Units of Theodore Roosevelt National Park offer comparably wonderful experiences. If you have the good fortune to visit both units, then you can make up your own mind about how they differ.

The Visitor Center Area

At the North Unit's small visitor center, you can watch either a thirteen-minute park film or a shorter three-minute park preview video. You can also view exhibits, look through a small bookstore run by the Theodore Roosevelt Nature & History Association, ask park staff any questions you have, and use the restroom. If you want to participate in an interpretive program led by a park staff member, then check here for a schedule of program times (summer only). After stopping at the visitor center, start your journey down the 14-mile park road—watch for wildlife on or near the road. The North Unit has a sizable herd of bison.

As you start down the park road, early views will allow you to enjoy the Little Missouri River's beauty. After about 2 miles of driving, you will arrive at the first stop, known as the Longhorn Pullout. Here you will see a landscape full of sagebrush and will also have the possibility of seeing the park's small herd of longhorn cattle. An interpretive sign provides information

Please use caution when driving in the park—bison often hang out on or near the park's roads.

about the longhorns and the history of cattle ranching in the badlands. Todd Stoeberl explains that "while we have Texas longhorns here, it wasn't a breed that Theodore Roosevelt ran. But during Roosevelt's time there was a ranch just north of the North Unit run by the Reynolds brothers, and they ran cattle from Texas through the park on what was called the Long X Trail. So the longhorns are here as a demonstration herd to remind us of North Dakota's important ranching history."

Continuing down the road for about another 0.5 mile, you will reach the Slump Block Pullout. The interpretive sign describes how water, sliding, and erosion help shape the look of the consistently layered buttes of the badlands. To help you better understand the geological process, the sign uses a nearby butte as an example. In another 2.5 miles you will reach the Cannonball Concretions Pullout and an intersection where you can turn left to go to Juniper Campground.

Juniper Campground

When entering the campground, you will first see a building on your right that sometimes is used as a residence by park staff. Outside the building you can find information about the park and campground. There is also a small parking area for those who want to take the Little Mo Trail. This 1.1-mile loop trail takes you near the river and has a nice interpretive brochure. Part of the trail is wheelchair accessible. For people who are not camping, a picnic area is available at the campground, as well as the last restrooms before heading farther west on the road.

Juniper Campground is the only established campground in the North Unit. It has beautiful trees and a scenic setting near the Little Missouri River. If you plan on camping, here are the essentials:

- The campground has 50 first-come, first-served sites.
- Six persons maximum are allowed to camp at any one campsite.
- A group site is available from May 1 to November 1 for groups of 6 to 60 persons. Reservations are accepted.
- The campground offers flush toilets and running water during the summer months, with picnic tables and grills at each site. There are no other amenities.
- There are numerous pull-through sites for trailers and RVs, and a dump station is available May through September. Generators are allowed from 8:00 A.M. to 8:00 P.M.

Juniper Campground offers a beautiful setting for relaxation and fun. Nearby Little Mo trail offers a short, easy walk for viewing the river.

- The campground is open year-round and rarely fills.
- In the summer months, park staff members present interpretive campfire programs at the campground amphitheater.
- Pets are allowed but must be on a leash less than 6 feet long. Pets cannot be left unattended or allowed to approach wildlife.

The Cannonball Concretions and Caprock Coulee Areas

Across from the road that leads to Juniper Campground is one of the North Unit's most interesting pullouts. The Cannonball Concretions Pullout allows you to see some interesting spherical rock formations that look like . . . well . . . cannonballs. An interpretive sign describes how they form. At this parking area, there is also access to the Buckhorn Trail. This 11.4-mile loop trail goes primarily through flat areas in the North Unit. It also goes

"Fire at will, captain!" Stop at the Cannonball Concretions Pullout to learn more about the geology behind these fascinating formations.

through one prairie dog town and near another, and it can be accessed at numerous points.

After taking time to marvel at the cannonball concretions, head down the road about a mile to the Long X Trail Pullout. Here an interpretive sign discusses the history of a trail that was used to drive cattle to the Long X Ranch. The ranch was located several miles north of this spot. This pullout is also a good place for you to take a moment and look at the slopes to the south and compare them with the slopes to the north. Are you seeing more trees to the south or on the north-facing slopes? Looking to the north, do you notice that the south-facing slopes have almost no trees? These differences can be attributed to how the sun's power dries out moisture from the soils of the south-facing slopes—thus allowing fewer trees to grow.

After-Dark Activities

If you are planning on camping in the park, or staying after dark, there are a few fun activities you might like to try. During the summer months, park staff offer interpretive programs on a variety of topics at the campground amphitheaters. They also sometimes offer night hikes, but you can do night hikes on your own as well. If you choose to do one, I recommend going on a trail you have already walked or in a familiar area that you used in the daytime. You should also not go alone and remember to take at least two sources of light. These precautions will help make sure you have a great experience. Notice what is different at night. Do you see or hear different animals? Do you notice any different smells? As time goes on, have your eyes adjusted so that can you see better in the dark?

Another possibility for a night activity is stargazing. Generally speaking, all you need for this activity is a clear sky. A telescope, book, or person who is knowledgeable about astronomy might enhance the experience. And don't forget about campfire activities like making s'mores, having sing-alongs, playing games, or practicing the art of storytelling. Maybe you can have a storytelling competition. Tell other people before your night gathering that they should come up with a story. The favorites at nighttime generally tend to be scary stories. But I have heard many other types of stories at outdoor night gatherings, told with great power and effect. Think ahead of time about the people you know who tell stories well. What makes them good storytellers? When you find the answer to this question, try to emulate these people. You will probably have great success.

Drive a little bit farther to reach the Caprock Coulee Trail parking area on your right. This parking area is the departure point for several hiking options. The Caprock Coulee Trail can be hiked as a 4.2-mile loop. There is a portion of the trail that you can hike in and hike out for a round-trip of 1.6 miles, using an interpretive brochure as your guide. You also can connect with the Buckhorn Trail at this parking area and make a flat 1.5-mile round-trip walk to the North Unit's most easily accessible prairie dog town. Once you leave this parking area, take note of the rugged, huge looking buttes you will see while driving the road up to the River Bend Overlook. The perspective you will get of these buttes while driving through them is a unique experience in the park. Would you want to try to *hike* through this area?

Park Geology: Non-Drowsy Formula

Do you have a hard time not falling asleep if someone starts talking about geology? Well, if you do, then this section is for you. Even though I have come across many geologists in my travels, I still have not met one who can successfully meet the challenge I offer them: Make geology interesting for me. Each one of them gets an excited smile when presented with the challenge and gives it their best try but ultimately does not succeed. If you are anything like me, you probably can appreciate when something looks beautiful or interesting. You also probably enjoy hearing a morsel of information about how that thing turned out that way. So I will keep my discussion of Badlands geology extremely brief.

The Little Missouri River Badlands have formed over millions of years in an area that was once covered by swamps and shallow water. Gradual climate changes, weather, erosion, fires, rivers, plants, dinosaurs, other animals, and people have changed and will continue to alter the look of things here. Today the most notable badlands feature are buttes that were created by the Little Missouri River; wind- and water-deposited sediments were later carved by the river's ebb and flow. Erosion and weather continue to sculpt the buttes, making what we see today. Valleys, grasslands, river bottoms, sagebrush flats, prairie dog towns, and thick vegetation on north-facing slopes are the surrounding cast for the buttes of the North Dakota badlands and help contribute to the region's scenic beauty.

Within the park you will find numerous geological formations of interest, like caprocks (on top of what are known as "rain pillars"), coal seams, petrified wood, concretions, and clinker. Some places I suggest going if you have an interest in geology are Wind Canyon and the Petrified Forest in the South Unit and the Cannonball Concretions Pullout, Caprock Coulee Trail, and Sperati Point in the North Unit.

If you feel utterly dissatisfied by this extremely short section (or with the other brief mentions of geological subjects in the book), a good resource is the *Roadlog Guide for the South & North Units*. The park's visitor centers also have some exhibits about the park's geology.

River Bend Overlook

I believe that the River Bend Overlook provides one of the best—if not the best—view in the North Unit. You get to enjoy a majestic overlook of the badlands and the Little Missouri River, while also admiring the charm of a

The River Bend Overlook affords one of the most gorgeous views in the park.

historic shelter built by the Civilian Conservation Corps. An interpretive sign at this overlook tells more about the shelter and its builders. For those who want to take a closer look, a short path leads to the shelter. The Caprock Coulee Trail intersects the road near the overlook and allows hikers also to enjoy the view.

The Oxbow Overlook Area

After driving about a mile farther down the road from the River Bend Overlook, you will come to the Bentonitic Clay Overlook. This overlook gives another view of the badlands and has an interpretive sign that tells about bentonitic clay. This type of clay is common in the badlands—and extremely slippery and messy to walk on when wet. If you hike almost any-

Can You Find the Bighorn Sheep?

In the North Unit of the park, you have the chance of seeing bighorn sheep. You will, however, have to be patient or very lucky. The current population of bighorn is small (around twenty animals), and they tend to stay up high on the buttes. These sheep are members of a species known as California bighorn and were reintroduced to the park in the 1990s as a replacement for the Audubon bighorn, an extinct species that once inhabited the area. Todd Stoeberl, the North Unit's district naturalist, says, "While I've seen sheep close to the visitor center at times, your best opportunities to see them are on the last 6 miles of the road, from the River Bend Overlook to the Oxbow Overlook. Use binoculars and look at the cliffs, and you might see them."

where in the backcountry, you are almost certain to come across it. One nice thing about the clay is that it does provide a good place for you to see animal tracks.

Beyond the Bentonitic Clay Overlook, you will quickly notice that the landscape you are driving through is different. You are now above the buttes and driving through flat, grassy plains. You will still be able to see the vastness of the badlands to the south. The Man and Grass Pullout has an interpretive sign that tells about how the abundant grass of the region was a major draw for cattle ranchers. Be sure to start looking for wildlife. The grassy areas around the pullout are a fantastic place to look for bison, deer, birds, and coyotes. I would be very surprised if you do not see deer while in this area of the North Unit. Also notice how in several places you can see the fence that surrounds the park. It is designed to keep bison within the park while allowing other animals to come and go.

In a few miles you will come to the Edge of Glacier Pullout. An interpretive sign tells about the large rocks you see on the ground. Geologists think these rocks were brought here from Canada thousands of years ago by an extremely large glacier. A little over a mile farther you will come to the end of the park road and the Oxbow Overlook. This overlook provides yet another excellent view of the Little Missouri River with the badlands as a backdrop. The river bends below in an oxbowlike fashion. One interpretive sign here explains the geology behind the creation of the oxbow in the river. Another recalls Theodore Roosevelt's famous chase after boat thieves. (This

The park has two species of deer: mule and white-tailed. You're more likely to see the less-elusive mule deer, like those in this photograph.

story is told in detail in the Visiting Elkhorn Ranch chapter.)

Adjacent to the Oxbow Overlook parking area, you will find a trailhead for the Achenbach Trail. This long loop trail (17.7 miles total) is a favorite of backpackers, as it offers many great views and a lot of solitude. For those interested in geology, or another view of the oxbow bend in the river, you can walk out to Sperati Point in a 2.2-mile round-trip hike through flat grasslands.

Four Cool Critters to Keep an Eye Out For

Each time I go out hiking in the park, it seems possible that I might come across an animal I haven't seen before. These creatures include a wide variety of reptiles, amphibians, insects, birds, small mammals, and fish. I want to mention a few animals of special interest.

The first are burrowing owls, which often live in prairie dog burrows and chase insects and other animals by running on the ground. They have developed a unique call that sounds similar to a rattlesnake's rattle. Why? They probably do it to fake predators out and help protect their nests and eggs.

The next cool critters are short-horned lizards. These small lizards have small spines and spots on their backs and eat insects. For defense they can inflate their bodies to show off their spines; they can also shoot blood out of their eyes!

Have you ever seen dung beetles? I've seen them on the park road. They roll dung into balls, lay eggs inside the balls, and then bury the balls. They are one of nature's great recyclers and help keep fly populations in check by burying dung before flies can lay their eggs.

Lastly there are turkey vultures, often misidentified as hawks or eagles. Identify them by their V-shaped tippy wings as they soar. They are one of the few North American birds with a sense of smell. They use it to locate decaying, dead animals—not to circle above animals that are about to die. (Appendix D includes a comprehensive list of the animals that live in the park.)

Camping, Lodging, and Services near the North Unit

The closest community to the North Unit where you can find lodging, supplies, food, or additional places to camp is Watford City (to the north), about a 15-mile drive from the park entrance. While the community is not as geared toward tourism as Medora is, it still appreciates visitors. There are also a few places to camp/stay and one place to eat south of the North Unit, near the small town of Grassy Butte. These options will be discussed first.

Grassy Butte Area

Grassy Butte is a very small town. Its population probably does not deviate far from around a couple hundred persons (and that's including people in surrounding areas). The only place to eat in Grassy Butte is at the Long X Saloon (think burgers and grilled food). One interesting place to stop and take a quick look is the Old Sod Post Office. This post office, which is now a small museum and a nationally registered historic site, was originally constructed in 1912 with sod and logs.

Camping

If the North Unit's Juniper Campground isn't your cup of tea, then maybe one of these options will work for you:

Bennett Campground (7 miles north of Grassy Butte, off US 85). USDA Forest Service campground; primitive camping. (701) 842–2393; www.fs.fed.us/rl/dakotaprairie/camping.htm.

Grassy Butte Community Park (US 85 South). 25 sites with hookups, picnic tables, grills; vault toilets, pay phones. (701) 863–6906.

Maah Daah Hey Trail Lodge (1744 Twentieth Street SW). Tent and RV camping (hookups available). Tent camping: (701) 225–6109; www.maah daahheylodge.com.

Lodging

The lodging options in the Grassy Butte area do not include motels and hotels, but there are some other intriguing choices.

The Bunkhouse (12942 Beicegel Creek Road). Fully furnished cabin sleeps 8. Hookups for campers; horse accommodations; nearby recreation and hunting opportunities. (701) 863–6721; www.4eyes.net/bunkhouse.

Lone Butte Ranch (11251 Lone Butte Road). Log cabins with fully furnished kitchens, electricity, bathrooms, linens; gas grill and hot tub on decks; horse boarding; quiet setting. (701) 863–6864 or (800) 546–4851; www.4eyes.net/lonebutte.

Maah Daah Hey Trail Lodge (1744 Twentieth Street SW). Bedrooms with full bath and kitchen; guide service available. (701) 225–6109; www.maahdaahheylodge.com.

Paradise Ridge Getaway (13311 Seventh Street NW). Cabin sleeps 6. (701) 863–6725.

Rock Creek Lodging and Shuttle (12872 Sixth Street NW). Ranch house with full kitchen, bathroom, electricity, AC, CATV, four bedrooms, linens, laundry; horse boarding. (701) 863–6768 or (800) 863–1495; www.maahdaahheylodging.com; e-mail: rchartman@ndsupernet.com.

Watford City Area

Watford City has a population of around 1,400, and there are several places that might be of interest to you. The Long X Trading Post (corner of US 85 South and West) offers a visitor center, pioneer museum, and gift shop.

You can get information and maps here as well as use the Internet. A new theater complex offers two movie screens. In summertime the Wild West Water Park (315 Third Street SE) might make a fun place to cool off in a pool, soothe your muscles in a hot tub, or ride down two different slides. The Watford City Municipal Golf Course (2 miles east of Watford City) is a nine hole course (call 701–842–2074 for rates). A small nature park (southeast area of Watford City) has a fishing pier and a four-acre pond stocked with perch, catfish, rainbow trout, and bluegills. McKenzie County Heritage Park (US 85 West) is open in summer and has some old buildings that interpret the region's pioneer heritage. For more information about things you can do in the Watford City area, visit www.4eyes.net/tourism. Camping, lodging, restaurants, and outfitters are described below.

Camping

CCC Campground (just south of North Unit, on U.S. Highway 85). USDA Forest Service campground; 17 sites with water; horse corrals available; Maah Daah Hey Trail access. (701) 842–2393; www.fs.fed.us/rl/dakotaprairie/camping.htm.

Cherry Creek Campground (east area of town). Tent and RV campground; 30 sites with hookups. (701) 444–3024.

McKenzie Bay Campground (40 miles east of Watford City). Tent and RV campground; some sites with hookups; swimming available. (701) 759–3366.

Prairieland RV Park (southwest area of town). RV sites with full hookups. (701) 842–2244 or (701) 770–6939.

Watford City Tourist Park (Highway 23 East). 12 RV sites with hookups. (701) 444–3457 or (701) 570–3677.

White Buffalo RV Park/Campground (east area of town). RV sites with full hookups. (701) 842–4839.

Woods RV and Trailer Park (east area of town). 25 RV Sites with full hookups. (701) 662–4913 or (701) 444–4120.

Lodging

Motels and Hotels

Four Eyes Motel (124 South Main Street, central area of town). 10 rooms, AC, CATV. (701) 444–4126.

McKenzie Inn (132 Southwest Third Street, central area of town). 13 rooms, AAA rated, CATV, refrigerators, free hookup for DSL. (701)

444–3980 or (800) 842–3989; www.mckenzieinn.com; e-mail: rmaki@ruggedwest.com.

Roosevelt Inn and Suites (on US 85 West). 50 rooms, AAA rated, free internet access; indoor pool, continental breakfast. (701) 842–3686 or (800) 887–9170; www.rooseveltinn.com; e-mail: mmulder@roosevelt inn.com.

Resorts and Cabins

Big Missouri Cabins (north of Watford City). Open April through October. Cabins sleep 4 to 6 adults and have full bathrooms. Cabins include refrigerator, microwave, electric skillet/crockpot, gas grill, cookware, linens, towels, TV/VCR. Horse corrals available; full RV hookup available for those with campers. (701) 842–2050 or (701) 842–3012; www.bigmissouricabins.com; e-mail: dm@bigmissouricabins.com.

Deep Creek Adventures (11010 Sixteenth Street NW). Cabins sleep 4 to 6 people. Guided hunting and ATV trips. (701) 759–3460; www.deep creekadventures.com; e-mail: BarURanch@deepcreekadventures.com.

Lazy A-H Cabin (4433 105th Avenue NW). Cabin with deck overlooking Lake Sakakawea and the badlands. Cabin has electricity. Horse corrals are available. (701) 675–2401.

Tobacco Garden Resort & Marina (28 miles north of Watford City, Highway 1806). Resort offers cabins, camping for tenters, and RV sites with hookups; store, restaurant, and docks. (701) 842–6931.

Restaurants

There are several restaurants in Watford City. Open daily throughout the year are the Dakotan Family Restaurant (US 85 West), Ginny's Family Restaurant (US 85 West), TJs Family Restaurant (US 85 South), and the Outlaws Bar and Grill. Each of these restaurants serves a variety of food like sandwiches, soups, salads, burgers, steaks, and pizza. The Twist Drive In (US 85 West) and several gas stations also offer fast-food options and snacks The new theater complex also has two places to eat.

Outfitters

Little Knife Outfitters offers guided horseback trail rides in the North Unit and on the Maah Daah Hey Trail. Also guided hunting trips, canoe rental, and shuttle services. For rates and information call (701) 842–2631 or visit www.littleknifeoutfitters.com; e-mail: littleknifeout fitters@hotmail.com.

Visiting Elkhorn Ranch

Bruce Kaye, Theodore Roosevelt National Park's chief of interpretation, explains that "the Elkhorn Ranch is a special spot. It's really kind of like the Walden Pond of the West. You can explore the Little Missouri River bottom, bird-watch, view wildlife, and, in total, you can really get the experiences that Roosevelt got—the ones that helped him get his conservation ethic. You can sit there and hear, as Roosevelt wrote, 'the trembling tremulous leaves of the cottonwood trees.' And you can see just how Roosevelt would have been sitting on the porch recording his feelings." Elkhorn Ranch was the second ranch that Roosevelt operated in the Little Missouri River Badlands. It became his base of operations as well as what he often called his "home ranch." The Elkhorn Ranch Unit of Theodore Roosevelt National Park is not an easy place to get to today. If you choose to visit, know that there is not a lot of physical evidence of the ranch remaining. Even if you do not choose to visit Elkhorn Ranch, you might enjoy reading the history of the ranch below and the story of Roosevelt's most famous adventure in the badlands.

Why Did Roosevelt Want a Second Ranch?

Roosevelt had numerous reasons for wanting to have a second ranch in North Dakota. One reason related to his desire to expand his cattle business,

While there are no longer any buildings at the Elkhorn Ranch Unit, a visit allows you to walk in Roosevelt's footsteps and ponder the importance of this place to conservation today.

as it seemed to be working out well. Another had to do with how Roosevelt liked to write; he did not find it easy to write with all the hustle and bustle at the Maltese Cross Ranch. He wanted to find a place where he could quietly write with few distractions. The final reason that Roosevelt wanted another ranch probably had to do with his desire to have more friends around. He was able to convince two friends from Maine, Wilmot Dow and Bill Sewall, to come work for him at what would eventually be the Elkhorn Ranch. Dow and Sewall had served as hunting guides for Roosevelt back in Maine, and he had the utmost respect for them. Some of Roosevelt's biographers note that Sewall was probably something of a father figure for Roosevelt. He would often be the person who soothed Roosevelt's worries after the tragic deaths of Roosevelt's first wife and his mother.

Roosevelt selected the location for his new ranch after riding through land north of his Maltese Cross Ranch. He ultimately chose a place that was 35 miles north of Medora, next to the Little Missouri River, and far from other people. Hermann Hagedorn, Roosevelt's primary biographer for the Badlands period, creates a romantic scene of how Roosevelt chose the spot and name for the ranch: "At the edge of the river he came upon the interlocked antlers of two elk who had died in combat. He determined that it was there that his 'home-ranch' should stand."

Roosevelt made one of his trips back east and brought Sewall and Dow back with him in 1884. Almost immediately they began cutting down cottonwood trees and started constructing the buildings for Roosevelt's new ranch. They finished in the summer of the following year, having built a large ranch house, a barn with stables, a shed, a blacksmith shop, and a chicken house.

One serious problem did occur while the ranch was being built. Because the land on which Roosevelt's ranch was being built was owned by the government, Roosevelt did not have anything more than squatter's rights to the land. While Sewall and Dow were building the ranch, they lived in a small

Roosevelt (center) brought Wilmot Dow (left) and Bill Sewall (right) out from Maine to help him build and operate his Elkhorn Ranch. THEODORE ROOSEVELT COLLECTION, HARVARD COLLEGE LIBRARY.

dugout cabin they had built. One of Medora's most seedy characters, E. G. Paddock, had a nasty habit of making claims to every old shack that existed out in the Badlands. Apparently, Paddock once arrived at the ranch with a drunken posse and ill intent. Roosevelt was away on a hunting trip, but Dow had the presence of mind to fix everyone a nice meal inside the ranch house while subtly showing them the vast array of weapons kept indoors. From that moment on, Paddock seemed less belligerent toward the men from Maine. But he apparently still had it in for Roosevelt and sought to gain some benefit from Roosevelt's "claims" to the land. Rumors circulated around the Badlands community that Paddock was going to shoot Roosevelt the first chance he got. When Roosevelt heard this news, he immediately rode to Paddock's house and confronted him. Roosevelt's words for Paddock were very blunt. Hagedorn quotes Roosevelt as saying, "'Paddock, I understand that you have threatened to kill me on sight. I have come over to see when you want to begin the killing and to let you know that, if you have anything to say against me, now is the time for you to say it.'" Paddock claimed that he had been "misquoted." This response apparently satisfied Roosevelt, concluding this particular episode with Paddock.

The ranch house that Sewall and Dow built for Roosevelt and themselves was, by the standards of the day, a mansion in the Badlands. The house was about 30 feet wide and 60 feet long. It had walls that were 7 feet high and eight rooms, a porch, and eighteen windows. In the basement was a dark room for developing photographs that Roosevelt took. In fact, most of the historic photographs we have of the ranch today were probably taken by Roosevelt.

While at the ranch, Roosevelt helped with the cattle business and also participated in several roundups. He also succeeded in his goal of writing more at Elkhorn. While he worked on his books about the Dakota Territory and hunting, the bulk of his time here was spent on a biography about Senator Thomas Hart Benton. Like many of Roosevelt's books, *A Life of Thomas Hart Benton* was a critical success. In addition to writing, Roosevelt found time to read while at the ranch. He owned a small library with historical books, some classics, and what we (or he!) would probably call "light reading." Elkhorn Ranch doesn't sound like a bad place, does it?

Sewall and Dow eventually brought their wives and Sewall's three-year-old daughter out to live at the Elkhorn. Two children were also born there. The addition of family to the setting made it feel more like home for everyone, Roosevelt included. It is probably likely though, that it also made Roosevelt yearn more for his own family.

In its time, Elkhorn Ranch was the epitome of fine living in the Dakota Territory.
THEODORE ROOSEVELT COLLECTION, HARVARD COLLEGE LIBRARY.

Roosevelt and the Boat Thieves

Roosevelt's most famous adventure in the Badlands occurred at the Elkhorn Ranch. In March 1886 the Little Missouri River was so icy that Roosevelt and his companions were unable to cross the river with horses. They used a boat instead. One morning the trio awoke to discover that the boat had been stolen. If Roosevelt did not pursue the boat thieves, he would set a bad precedent. Reputation was everything to Roosevelt, and he wanted to make it clear that he would not tolerate having his property stolen.

Who were the thieves? Roosevelt suspected that three men who lived in a shack about 20 miles to the north were responsible. These men were of ill repute and were the only other group nearby known to own a boat capable of getting them to the Elkhorn. Sewall suggested that they build a boat and pursue the thieves. Roosevelt liked this idea, and in three days the boat was ready.

Taking provisions with them, Roosevelt and his men from Maine took off into the cold to pursue the thieves. The trio suffered through the howling wind and terrible cold. Roosevelt took a thermometer that showed that the temperature dropped to 0 degrees Fahrenheit. He also took some books with him and possibly a camera. On the third day, about 50 miles downstream (near Cherry Creek) they spotted their boat. It was tied to the shore, and smoke from a campfire indicated that the thieves were nearby. The heroes crept up on the camp and quickly captured the one person who was there. Around sunset the other culprits returned from hunting and were also taken by surprise. Roosevelt told them that if they tried anything they would be shot, but otherwise they would be okay. His mind was set on bringing the thieves to justice.

The next day, captors and captives continued downriver. The river became so icy that travel was impossible. Roosevelt spent his waiting time reading Tolstoy's *Anna Karenina* as well as the writings of Matthew Arnold. Roosevelt also read a book that was in the possession of the thieves—*The History of the James Brothers*. Roosevelt enjoyed the irony of reading an account of some of history's more successful thieves.

Several days later, the river was still frozen, the men were almost out of food, and something needed to be done. Roosevelt borrowed supplies and a horse from nearby ranchers. He also hired a man with a wagon. He left Sewall and Dow with fresh supplies and the boats and headed out with the wagon to bring the thieves to justice. For two days he marched behind the wagon with his gun, all the way to Dickinson, Dakota Territory. The thieves were put in jail, and two of the three were later convicted. Sewall and Dow took the boats down the river to Mandan, Dakota Territory, where they then shipped their boats back to Medora by train.

It would be an understatement to say that people were impressed by Roosevelt's resolve. As an additional tribute to Roosevelt's ability to impress and get people to like him, one of the thieves later wrote him a letter from jail to apologize for taking the boat. He also said that he would greatly enjoy a visit from Roosevelt if he was ever around the Bismarck, North Dakota, penitentiary.

As a note of interest, there is some dispute about the photograph I have included in the The Life of Theodore Roosevelt chapter, which shows Roosevelt sitting with a gun, guarding the thieves. Until recently this photograph was thought to be a "live" photo of the action. But Dow's grandson has revealed a letter of Dow's that indicates this photograph was in fact a reenactment, with Dow and Sewall playing the roles of the captives. Additional information suggests that Roosevelt was not actually in the image either!

Elkhorn Ranch Today

During the terrible winter of 1886–87, Roosevelt lost most of his cattle to the cold. While he maintained ownership of the Maltese Cross Ranch, he decided to give up the Elkhorn around 1890. He probably visited the ranch for the last time in 1892. Six years later he sold the ranch to Sylvane Ferris. Only three years later, every piece of the buildings at the Elkhorn had been taken or destroyed.

As far as the Badlands go, I personally do not think the Elkhorn Ranch site has more inherent beauty than other places. The history of the place is what makes it intriguing. Today you can see a few cornerstones that mark where the buildings stood, but little else save the landscape. As Bruce Kaye says, "It was very likely that the Elkhorn was where Roosevelt penned the words 'It's not what we have that will make us a great nation, it's the way that we use it.'" A bulletin board here contains some historic photographs of the ranch, information about the Elkhorn buildings, and some quotations from Roosevelt and his companions.

Getting to Elkhorn Ranch

To get to the Elkhorn Ranch, you will need to stop by one of the park visitor centers to get a map. Plan to spend at least half a day making this journey. Regardless of which route you take, a short hike is required to get to the Elkhorn Ranch site. Below you will find a general overview for each route. You must check road conditions for any of the routes with park staff and get a map before embarking on a journey to this unit of the park.

From the East

Prior to 2007 the Elkhorn Ranch could be accessed from the east. This access involved crossing private property. However, ownership of the property has changed hands and, as of the time of this writing, the new owner had not granted permission for the public to cross private land. Please check with park staff for any updates on eastern access and also for directions to the Elkhorn via the western route.

From the West

Accessing the Elkhorn Ranch from the west allows you to reach the ranch site without having to ford the Little Missouri River. However, it is easy to get lost. I recommend following the map you get from park staff with extreme care. You will be on dirt roads, and you will need to watch for large oil trucks—oil well operations are common in this part of North Dakota. In total, it is about 45 miles from Medora to the Elkhorn parking area but takes about ninety minutes one-way. From Medora you will start by driving west on Interstate 94, exiting in a little more than 15 miles at Camel Hump Lake. Next head north while following the map. Near the end of your journey, you will pass the USDA Forest Service Elkhorn Camp, which provides the closest place to camp if you're going to the Elkhorn Ranch. Once you arrive at the parking area, you will see a bulletin board and registration box. Make your way through the fence and follow the grass trail north for about 0.6 mile to the Elkhorn Ranch site.

Walk Softly and Carry a Big Stick: Enjoying the Park's Backcountry

Theodore Roosevelt popularized a West African proverb: "Speak softly and carry a big stick; you will go far." While Roosevelt described a philosophical stance that came to represent an integral part of his character, the proverb has meaning when visiting the backcountry of Theodore Roosevelt National Park. While you should make as little impact as possible upon the park and its resources, you should also come well prepared for any journey you take into the backcountry. What do I mean by "backcountry"? The term refers to anywhere in the park that you can only reach on foot or on horseback. This chapter will tell you the most important things you need to know about hiking or horseback riding in the park's backcountry. It also contains descriptions of the park's trails.

Safety and Important Things to Know

How can you have a memorable and safe backcountry experience? As Tom Cox, the park's chief of resource and visitor protection, explains: "There are two key things you need in order to have a safe backcountry experience. Number one is to make sure you carry enough water. It's definitely the biggest concern and can cause serious problems for people who are unprepared. It can get very hot here in the summer, and hiking or other physical activity can increase the risk of dehydration even in mild weather. Number two is to know where you are and have a map or other reliable information with you that allows you to safely navigate from point A to point B." As Cox notes, water is extremely important in the park. There are no safe and reliable sources of potable water in the park's backcountry, so you will need to carry all of your water with you—and take plenty. It's very easy to get dehydrated in the backcountry. One gallon of water per person per day is recommended.

Some of the truly fun and amazing experiences you can have in the park result from the ability to go anywhere that looks intriguing to you. In other words, you do not have to stay on the trails while in the backcountry. When taking trails, I typically use them as my conduit for getting to areas of the park that I want to explore. There are trails even off the main trails. Bison and other animals make countless wildlife trails that can be easily confused with human-made trails. Park Ranger Kane Seitz adds that "the trails erode every time it rains, and with the wild horses and bison traffic it's impossible to maintain them."

For these reasons, if you want to hike a trail in its entirety, you need to be prepared to potentially lose the "actual" trail at various points. In fact, you should count on it happening. But don't worry. If you take a detailed map with you (a topographic map is best), then you will be able to locate where you are. In addition, the park's landscapes are out in the open, and there are usually trail markers that will help you from getting too lost. Once again—proper preparation is key.

Another aspect of traveling in the park's backcountry relates to bentonitic clay. When wet, this clay is sticky and is sometimes referred to as "gumbo." It is easy to get stuck in, is very messy, and possesses a legendary power to induce cartoonlike banana-peel slipping. The drier it is, the easier the clay is to walk across. One positive aspect to bentonitic clay is its ability to retain tracks. The park is a great place to learn more about animal tracks, as you will have regular access to them.

If there has been rain or snow in the park recently, be sure to ask about trail conditions. In addition to the challenges posed by bentonitic clay, creeks and the Little Missouri River can become serious obstacles. Some trails require creek or river crossings, so you will need to check ahead and make sure that it is safe for you to attempt the journey. To quote Seitz, "You just can't ride or hike in this type of country when it's wet."

The weather can change rapidly at any time of the year in the park. Winters can be exceptionally cold and summers exceptionally hot. If staying overnight in the backcountry, take a mix of clothing and camping accessories that will allow you to stay safe and comfortable in a diverse range of conditions. Also be aware that you need to give wildlife their space and the right-of-way. Any animal can be a threat to your safety if you do not treat it appropriately. Look out for prairie rattlesnakes, ticks, and poison ivy.

To camp overnight in the park's backcountry, you will need to get a free backcountry permit from either the South Unit's Medora Visitor Center or the North Unit's visitor center. There are currently no established backcountry campsites, so you will pick where you want to camp. You are limited to staying for fourteen nights total in the backcountry.

Please make yourself familiar with the backcountry regulations listed below. They will answer additional questions that you may have about use of the backcountry. Information specific to horseback riding follows in its own section.

Backcountry Regulations

The following list of regulations is printed courtesy of Theodore Roosevelt National Park.

1. All plants, wildlife, and natural and cultural features in the park are protected. Do not disturb or remove them. Collection of anything, including skulls, antlers, and other animal parts, is prohibited. Hunting is prohibited, as is the feeding or molesting of wildlife.
2. Chasing or otherwise harassing wildlife, including approaching wildlife on horseback, is prohibited.
3. Pets, bicycles, and motorized equipment are not permitted in the backcountry.
4. Firearms, fireworks, and explosives are not allowed in the park.
5. Open fires (wood, charcoal, etc.) are not permitted in the backcountry. Cooking must be done on a self-contained stove fueled by a commercial product. Use of stoves may be restricted in times of high fire danger.

6. All trash and other material packed in, including toilet paper, must be packed out. Burying or burning trash is not permitted.

7. Backcountry camping is prohibited within 0.25 mile of roads and trailheads and within 200 feet of any water source. Do not wash dishes or use detergents in water sources.

8. For proper sanitation, bury human waste in a shallow hole that is at least 6 to 8 inches deep and 200 feet or more from water sources.

9. Be considerate of others. Keep noise low. Hikers must yield the right-of-way to horseback riders.

10. Overnight parties in the backcountry are limited to a maximum of 10 persons without horses, or 8 persons and 8 horses.

Horseback Riding

Horseback riding in the park will allow you to experience the badlands much like Roosevelt did. Park Ranger Kane Seitz speculates that horseback riding in the park may be starting to equal or even eclipse hiking as the most popular activity. As with hiking, you can go anywhere you like when horseback riding, with several exceptions. You are not allowed to go into the developed campgrounds or picnic areas, ride on the roads, or go on the shorter, developed nature trails (Wind Canyon, Ridgeline, Coal Vein, Little Mo, and Painted Canyon). Grazing is prohibited, and all riders must use certified weed-free hay/feed to help prevent the spread of exotic plants.

If you own your own horses and want to stay overnight in the frontcountry, you can make a reservation to stay at the South Unit's Roundup Horse Camp. You can also stay at the Roundup Horse Camp if you do not have horses and plan on camping at the park with a large group. This campground has a loading ramp, a hitch rail, corrals, and water tanks for horses. In addition, there is a fire pit, drinking water, cooking grills, and a shelter with picnic tables. The area is locked, and a combination or key to the Roundup Horse Camp gate must be picked up at the South Unit entrance station.

Maximum group sizes are as follows: 20 people and 20 horses, or 30 people without horses. Your length of stay at the Roundup Horse Camp is limited to five nights over the course of a year. The campground is generally open May through October, although dates can vary.

You can make a reservation to use the Roundup Horse Camp on the first Monday of March. Requests must be mailed or faxed to the park; telephone reservations are not accepted. Requests postmarked before the first Monday in March will be discarded. It is not uncommon for the park to receive more requests than can be accommodated. To obtain a reservation form, call (701) 623–4466 or check the park's Web site. If you want to stay with your horses near the North Unit, your best bet is the CCC campground just south of its entrance.

For overnight trips in the backcountry, horse users must follow all the regulations listed above. When not mounted, horses must be secured using a hobble or by other means to protect trees and shrubs. It is also suggested that horseback riders maintain a distance of at least 300 yards from any bison or wild horses.

If you are interested in going on a guided horse ride, there are several options. Peaceful Valley Ranch is located in the heart of the South Unit and is operated by Shadow Country Outfitters (701–623–4568 or 701–677–4260). They offer trail rides, and prices vary based on the duration of your trip. All riders are required to be age seven or above, be at least 54 inches tall, and weigh less than 240 pounds. Different rides are available, including evening rides and trips for experienced riders.

The Medora Riding Stables (800–633–6723; www.medora.com) also offer rides in the badlands. Little Knife Outfitters (701–842–2631; www.littleknifeoutfitters.com) offers trail rides in the North Unit. Some accommodations near the park offer horseback riding trips as well.

Trail Descriptions
South Unit Trails

Buck Hill Trail

Distance: 0.1 mile one-way

Finding the trailhead: Starting from Medora, enter the South Unit of the park and continue straight on the park's loop road for about 17 miles. Shortly thereafter, turn right on a road that leads to the top of Buck Hill. The trail begins from the parking lot at the end of the road.

The hike: Most likely named for the numerous deer that live in the park, at 2,855 feet Buck Hill is the second highest point in the South Unit. Peck Hill, located near Painted Canyon, is 2,865 feet—just 10 feet higher. From a circular parking area, a somewhat steep 0.1-mile trail leads up to a ridge that is effectively the top of Buck Hill. The ridge offers some nice views of the surrounding areas but can be very windy. You get what is probably the only 360-degree view of the park here (if you choose not to go into the backcountry, that is). Once you are on the ridge, get your bearings by looking for a communications tower near the east entrance of the park and the Painted Canyon Visitor Center. For those who want to go a bit farther, the ridge continues for 0.2 mile.

Skyline Vista Trail

Distance: 0.1 mile one-way

Finding the trailhead: Starting from Medora, enter the South Unit of the park and continue straight on the park's loop road for about 4 miles, just past the first prairie dog town you see on top of Johnson Plateau. Look for a trail sign, and immediately turn left into a parking lot. The trail begins here.

The hike: The Skyline Vista Trail is a short, wheelchair-accessible trail that leads you to an interesting view of the Badlands. From here you can see three major buttes in the distance. The one farthest to your right (west) with the towers is Sentinel Butte. Square Butte is in the middle, and Bullion Butte is on the left.

Wind Canyon Loop Trail

Distance: 0.5-mile loop

Finding the trailhead: Starting from Medora, enter the park and continue clockwise on the loop road for about 6.5 miles, passing Cottonwood Campground. Take a left on the road that continues north toward Peaceful Valley Ranch. In about 4 miles you will reach the parking area for Wind Canyon and the trail.

The hike: Wind Canyon is a place where you can see geological forces in action. The short trail offers an interpretive sign that discusses the interesting wind- and water-made sandstone shapes you can see here. There is also a fantastic view of the Little Missouri River bending below as it heads north toward the South Unit's boundary. To get this view, make sure that you walk up to the trail to the north, and to the viewing area designated by a log fence. This location is a fantastic place for watching the sunset, and you might even hear the evening howl of coyotes.

Wind Canyon's wind- and water-sculpted sandstone geological formations make it one of the do-not-miss destinations in the park.

Ridgeline Nature Trail

Distance: 0.8-mile loop

Finding the trailhead: Starting from Medora, enter the South Unit of the park and continue straight on the park's loop road for about 11 miles. Look for a parking area and sign about 1.5 miles beyond the Scoria Point Overlook.

The hike: A self-guided brochure helps explain some of the features you will see on the Ridgeline Nature Trail. The trail has a variation of flat parts, as well as short uphill and downhill segments. You start the hike with a steep walk through dense vegetation for 0.1 mile. Once you are on top of the ridge (where there is a bench), you will see a junction with a spur trail to the right. You should go straight here as well as when you reach the next spur trail, where you could go right. At 0.4 mile you will reach the trail's culminating viewpoint before heading back on the loop toward where you began.

Old East Entrance

Distance: 0.4 mile one-way

Finding the trailhead: To get to the Old East Entrance, start from Medora and enter the South Unit of the park. Continue straight on the park's loop road for about 13 miles. Park in the small semicircle parking area located near Mile Marker 13. You can see the old entrance station from the pullout. There is no defined trail here, so you will need to head straight (east) into a prairie dog town. Walk through it toward a small clump of green trees in the distance. Look for the clump of trees that is farthest to the left in your view. As you walk closer, it will become more apparent where the building is located.

The hike: The Old East Entrance is a place to visit if you are interested in the park's history. This entrance was built in the mid-1930s by the Works Project Administration with the help of Albert E. Boicourt, who served as a stone mason and was also an early homesteader in an area that became part of the South Unit. After Interstate 94 was constructed in the mid-1960s, it was necessary for the park to make a new entrance, and the Old East Entrance was closed. Today you can still see the beautiful stonework of the old entrance building and the park's decorative stone gate. There is no defined trail for you to follow to get to the Old East Entrance, but it's pretty easy to find.

Coal Vein Nature Trail

Distance: 0.8-mile loop

Finding the trailhead: Starting from Medora, enter the South Unit of the park and continue straight on the park's loop road for about 15.5 miles. Take a right at the trail sign onto a road that leads to a parking area. The trail begins here.

The hike: This trail begins with an interpretive sign that explains how a small fire burned continuously in this area from 1951 to 1977. The fire started in a coal vein and just kept going, attracting hoards of tourists for many years. According to a self-guided brochure you can pick up in the parking area, visitors sometimes enjoyed roasting marshmallows over the

The beautiful stonework of the park's Old East Entrance, built in the 1930s, can still be seen today.

fire. The trail itself is primarily flat. Starting from the parking area, take the trail you see near the interpretive sign that tells about the burning coal vein. The path will eventually loop you back to where you begin. At 0.2 mile you will come to the point where the coal seam fire ended. Shortly thereafter you will view a small gorge filled with trees, briefly descend into it, and then walk back up out the other side. At 0.4 mile you get to the location where the coal vein fire actually started—but there is little evidence here or at the point where the fire terminated that will be easily recognizable. At 0.7 mile there is an interesting large piece of clinker (a brick-colored type of rock), just before the trail loops you back to where you began.

Painted Canyon Nature Trail

Distance: 0.9-mile loop

Finding the trailhead: From Medora, drive east on Interstate 94 for about 7 miles to exit 32 (the Painted Canyon exit). The trail begins on the west side of the visitor center, near the picnic shelter.

The hike: This steep loop trail descends from the western side of the Painted Canyon Visitor Center area and takes you to the canyon's floor, where you will get a different perspective on the colorful buttes of the badlands. The trail is not well maintained and can be slippery when wet. Despite its drawbacks, the trail has its rewards. In addition to its views, the trail journeys through some small groves of trees and displays excellent plant diversity. In summer and autumn I have observed a wide variety of wildflowers and shrubs growing around and near this trail. If you are passing by the park on the interstate and don't have time to enter the rest of the South Unit, this trail will provide you with a great introduction to the park. Make sure you have thirty minutes to one hour, and make sure that you don't mind the trail's steep beginning and end.

Painted Canyon Trail

Distance: 2.0 miles one-way

Finding the trailhead: From Medora, drive east on I–94 for about 7 miles to exit 32 (the Painted Canyon exit). The trail begins off a service road located on the east side of the visitor center.

The hike: This steep trail starts near the Painted Canyon Visitor Center and leads to an intersection in the middle of the Upper Paddock Creek Trail.

Mike Auney Trail

Distance: 3.0 miles one-way

Finding the trailhead: Starting from Medora, enter the park and continue straight on the loop road for about 6.5 miles, passing Cottonwood Campground. Take a left onto the road that heads north toward Peaceful Valley Ranch. In about 4 miles you will reach Wind Canyon. Continue for a short distance, and then go straight on East River Road. (Do not turn right on the loop road.) Continue on East River Road until you reach the road to your left that leads to the Roundup Horse Camp. If you are not staying at Roundup, you will most likely need to park your car nearby, as the gate may be locked. (Do not park in the road or block the gate.) Walk down the road. The trail begins from inside the horse camp.

The hike: The Mike Auney Trail serves as a connector trail between the Roundup Horse Camp and the Petrified Forest Loop Trail. Taking this trail requires fording the Little Missouri River and should only be attempted if conditions are safe. Mike Auney and his family were homesteaders who at one point lived near Jules Creek. Jules Creek parallels the South Unit's loop road.

Jones Creek Trail

Distance: 3.6 miles one-way

Finding the trailhead: This trail has eastern and western trailheads. The trail description provided above goes from west to east.

Western trailhead: Enter the park from Medora and continue straight on the loop road for about 6.5 miles, passing Cottonwood Campground. Turn left onto the road that continues north toward Peaceful Valley Ranch. Travel for about 1.5 miles farther; the trail's parking area is on your right.

Eastern trailhead: Enter the park from Medora and continue straight on the loop road for about 6.5 miles, passing Cottonwood Campground. Turn left onto the road that continues north toward Peaceful Valley Ranch. In about 4 miles you will come to an intersection (just past Wind Canyon); turn right to stay on the loop road. Continue about 4.2 miles; the parking area for the eastern end of the Jones Creek Trail is on your right.

The hike: One of Medora's most famous characters was a man known as "Hell-Roarin'" Bill Jones. A gunslinger, Jones was described by Hermann Hagedorn as "a striking creature, a man who could turn dreams into nightmares, merely by his presence in them." Hagedorn explains that Jones was also liked for his sass and storytelling ability: "He could build a yarn that had the architectural completeness of a turreted castle, created out of smoke by some imaginative minstrel of hell." I should mention that at one point Jones was a police officer in Bismarck, North Dakota. The job ended one day when Jones decided to hit the mayor on the head with his gun.

Initially Theodore Roosevelt did not like Bill Jones, and for good reason. According to hearsay, Roosevelt, in his own bold style told him, "Bill Jones, I can't tell why in the world I like you, for you're the nastiest-talking man I ever heard." Jones apparently apologized to Roosevelt, and they became friends. Jones would boast of his friendship with Roosevelt for the rest of his life and seemed to take some comfort in it even during his very last days. Roosevelt had that kind of effect on people.

Jones Creek Trail is most likely named for Bill Jones. Someone with a good sense of humor must have named the trail to complement the adjacent Lower Paddock Creek Trail, which also gets its name from a local misfit. The Jones Creek Trail is, for the most part, a flat trail. It begins at a parking area

The Jones Creek Trail was probably named for a famous gunslinger.

near where a Civilian Conservation Corps camp once was located. An interpretive sign in the parking area discusses the role of the CCC in the park.

After some hiking and beautiful scenery, at 0.9 mile you get what will be your first view of the trickle that is Jones Creek. At this point you will have to start crossing the creek on numerous occasions. The trail gets particularly hard to follow in several places, but if you keep heading in the same direction (between the buttes), you will eventually find your way. At 2.0 miles you will reach the intersection with Roundup Camp Trail that heads to the north. At 2.7 miles you will reach the junction with the Lower Talkington Trail that heads to the southeast. Near the end of the trail (by its eastern trailhead and parking area), you will walk by an interesting sandstone formation.

Upper Talkington Trail

Distance: 4.0 miles one-way

Finding the trailhead: This trail has eastern and western trailheads. The western trailhead is much easier to reach.

Western trailhead: Starting from Medora, enter the South Unit of the park and continue straight on the park's loop road for about 17.5 miles. Soon after you pass the road that leads to Buck Hill, start looking for a trail sign. Park; the trailhead is on the right side of the road. (The trail on the left is the *Lower* Talkington Trail.)

Eastern trailhead: You will need to ask park staff members where to go and where to park. Plan on using a map. Take I–94 west from Medora about 10 miles to exit 36 (Fryburg) and head north. After parking, you will need to slip under the park's fence to access the trailhead.

The hike: The Upper Talkington Trail lies to the east of the park's loop road and is for the most part flat. It has some creek crossings and culminates at the South Unit's eastern border. I've primarily used this trail from its eastern trailhead, which leads to some intriguing places that are rarely visited. I have fond memories of this trail, which has served as my departure point for getting to some of my favorite areas in the park. The eastern part of the trail goes near a prairie dog town, where I've seen pronghorn, bison, elk, coyotes, rabbits, and prairie rattlesnakes. (Also see the Lower Talkington Trail description.)

Lower Talkington Trail

Distance: 4.1 miles one-way

Finding the trailhead: This trail's western end begins as an intersection with the Jones Creek Trail. The eastern trailhead (directions provided here) is located on the park's loop road. Starting from Medora, enter the South Unit of the park and continue straight on the park's loop road for about 17.5 miles. Soon after you pass the road that leads to Buck Hill, start looking for a trail sign. Park; the trailhead is on the left side of the road. (The trail on the right is the *Upper* Talkington Trail.)

The hike: The Talkington Trails cover a large part of the park's eastern areas. The Talkingtons were a family who once owned an area of what is now the South Unit. The Lower Talkington Trail is west of the park loop road; the Upper Talkington Trail is east of the park loop road. The Lower Talkington Trail takes you over a range of topography and involves crossing some creeks. A segment of the trail can be combined with the Jones Creek and Lower Paddock Creek Trails to make a large loop. The trail has a lot of bentonitic clay.

Roundup Camp Trail

Distance: 4.4 miles one-way

Finding the trailhead: Starting from Medora, enter the park and continue straight on the loop road for about 6.5 miles, passing Cottonwood Campground. Turn left onto the road that heads north toward Peaceful Valley Ranch. In about 4 miles you will reach Wind Canyon. Continue for a short distance, and then go straight onto East River Road. (Do not turn right on the loop road.) Continue on East River Road until you reach the road to your left that leads to the Roundup Horse Camp. If you are not staying at Roundup, you will most likely need to park your car nearby, as the gate may be locked. Look for a trail that leads away from the horse camp to the southeast.

The hike: This trail leads from the Roundup Horse Camp to an intersection in the middle of the Jones Creek Trail.

Lower Paddock Creek Trail

Distance: 4.2 miles one-way

Finding the trailhead: This trail has eastern and western trailheads.

Eastern trailhead: Starting from Medora, enter the park, and continue straight on the loop road for about 14.4 miles. The trail is marked by a sign near a culvert on the park road. The parking area is about 0.25 mile to the north.

Western trailhead: Starting from Medora, enter the park and continue straight on the loop road for about 6.5 miles, passing Cottonwood Campground. Turn left onto the road that heads north toward Peaceful Valley Ranch. Travel a little over 0.5 mile and turn right onto a dirt road. At the end of this road, you will find a parking area and a prairie dog town where the trail begins.

The hike: This trail is one of my favorites in the park. Its western end begins in a prairie dog town and will take you through several others as you walk near and over Paddock Creek. The trail contains plenty of short, slick dips and more than ten creek crossings. These crossings will most certainly make for a muddy experience when wet, but they can also be very dry.

A man named E. G. Paddock once owned a cabin near the creek, and the creek and trail are named after him. He was a terrible person by all accounts and yet managed to survive and even prosper in Medora. He guided many of the hunters who came to the badlands. He was also known to be a murderer, horse thief, and cattle thief and generally was considered the kingpin of all fraudulent activities in Medora. He spread rumors that he was going to shoot Roosevelt but backed down after Roosevelt confronted him. Roosevelt did not keep a grudge though. Years later, after becoming the governor of New York, Roosevelt thanked Paddock for lending him a rifle and hammer when he first came to Medora to hunt bison.

Upper Paddock Creek Trail

Distance: 7.7 miles one-way

Finding the trailhead: This trail has eastern and western trailheads; the western trailhead is much easier to get to.

Western trailhead: Start from Medora and enter the park. Drive straight on the loop road for about 14.5 miles. Look for a sign near a culvert on the road; this is where the trail begins. The parking area is located about 0.25 mile farther down the road. If you have reached the road that goes to the Coal Vein Trail, you have gone too far.

Eastern trailhead: You will need to ask park staff members where to go and where to park. Plan on using a map. Take I–94 west from Medora about 10 miles to exit 36 (Fryburg) and head north. After parking, you will need to slip under the park's fence to access the trailhead.

The hike: This trail meanders along the eastern areas of the park and like its sister trail, requires some creek crossings. The trail ends near the southeast corner of the South Unit. It also intersects the Painted Canyon Trail 3.3 miles east of its western trailhead. (Also see the Lower Paddock Creek Trail description.)

Petrified Forest Loop Trail

Distance: Various

Finding the trailhead: Ask park staff members for directions to the Petrified Forest. If you're approaching from the west, it is important to get an up-to-date map and directions from park personnel. If you're approaching from the east, you need to find out if it is safe to cross the Little Missouri River.

The hike: The Petrified Forest Loop Trail travels through the Theodore Roosevelt Wilderness Area in the South Unit and allows you to see large pieces of petrified wood. The trail can be reached from the western boundary of the park or from the east, starting near the Peaceful Valley Ranch. Most visitors choose to reach the forest from the west, because fording the Little Missouri River and a longer trip are required if approaching from the east. Entering from the west, it is possible to do part of the trail in a round-trip of about 3 miles and see a popular area that contains many pieces of petrified wood. To do that short trip, ask park staff for a map and directions at one of the visitor centers. One important thing to understand about using any route to get to the Petrified Forest is that if it has rained recently, bentonitic clay will make the trails nearly impassable. It is imperative that you check road and trail conditions with park staff before attempting a trip to the Petrified Forest. The loop trail in its entirety from the west is 10.7 miles round-trip. From the east the loop is 15.3 miles round-trip. A section of the loop is also part of the Maah Daah Hey Trail.

Lone Tree Loop Trail

Distance: Various

Finding the trailhead: As with the Petrified Forest system of trails, ask park personnel for directions if you plan on accessing this trail from Medora.

The hike: This trail is located in the Petrified Forest area of the park but also can be reached from Medora. Part of the trail passes Knutson Creek, the only major body of water in the park west of the Little Missouri River. If you start from Medora, the loop is 15.3 miles. From the western boundary of the park, the loop totals 10.7 miles.

Maah Daah Hey Trail

Distance: 96.0 miles

The hike: This exciting trail connects all three units of the park. It can be biked, hiked, or done on horseback. It deserves its own section and discussion, which appear in the Nearby Excursions and Recreation Opportunities chapter. *Note:* Bicycles are not permitted on the Maah Daah Hey Trail within the park.

Battleship Butte can be seen from the Little Mo Nature Trail. Can you figure out how the butte got its name?

North Unit Trails

Little Mo Nature Trail

Distance: 0.7-mile or 1.1-mile loop

Finding the trailhead: The trail is located at the entrance to Juniper Campground. To reach the campground, enter the North Unit of the park and head straight for about 4.5 miles. Turn left, going toward the campground. You will see a building on your right that sometimes serves as a residence for park staff. Parking is available on the left-hand side of the building. The trail begins across the road.

The hike: The Little Mo Trail is an easy loop trail that takes you near the Little Missouri River and then up a small butte to give you a slightly better vantage point for viewing the river and Juniper Campground. This fairly flat nature trail is paved for a little more than half its distance, making it an accessible trail. A self-guided brochure provides some simple information about features on the trail, as well as information about some of the park's plants and animals. Highlights include a Civilian Conservation Corps–built picnic shelter, a view of Battleship Butte, and some rain pillars and caprocks. You can pick up the brochure at the trailhead.

Trail to Sperati Point

Distance: 1.1 miles one-way

Finding the trailhead: After entering the North Unit, drive to the end of the road (13.7 miles) and park at the Oxbow Overlook. The trail, a segment of the Achenbach Trail, begins here.

The hike: The Little Missouri River once headed to the north and joined other rivers to drain into Hudson Bay, in northeastern Canada. During the last ice age the river was blocked from flowing north. The river eventually cut through the Achenbach Hills at Sperati Point and turned east in an oxbowlike fashion. Today the Little Missouri River connects to a different system of rivers and eventually drains into the Gulf of Mexico.

In a practical sense, walking out to Sperati Point does not give you vivid evidence of the Little Missouri River bursting through the Achenbach Hills. What you do get is another nice view of the river and Oxbow Bend. The hike itself is actually part of the Achenbach Trail and is flat and easy until you get to the end. Start the walk from the Oxbow Overlook parking lot, and take a right (or head south and to the west) on the Achenbach Trail at the trail register. At 0.9 mile there is a trail junction. Keep going straight for a little more than 0.1 mile until you reach the viewpoint and you have reached Sperati Point.

Trail to Prairie Dog Town

Distance: 0.75 mile one-way

Finding the trailhead: After entering the North Unit, drive 6.2 miles to the Caprock Coulee Trail parking lot. You will start the walk here.

The hike: The easiest way to get to one of the North Unit's three prairie dog towns is to hike a short segment of the Buckhorn Trail, starting from the Caprock Coulee trailhead. From the junction at the start of the primary Caprock Coulee trailhead, head right (east). At the next junction take a left (head north). This flat trail goes quickly and will allow you to observe prairie dogs, one of the park's most interesting animals.

Caprock Coulee Trail

Distance: 4.2-mile loop

Finding the trailhead: The Caprock Coulee Trail can be accessed from several locations. For the first possible access, enter the North Unit and drive 6.2 miles to the Caprock Coulee Trail parking lot. The trail can also be accessed at the River Bend Overlook, an additional 1.6 miles down the park road.

The hike: The Caprock Coulee Trail has a segment that is north of the park road and a segment that is south of the park road. The trail has a self-guided brochure for its first 0.8 mile. This short self-guided segment is known as the Caprock Coulee Nature Trail and concludes where you can see some caprocks and rain pillars. After this point the trail continues, gets more rigorous and ends up at the park road near the River Bend Overlook after 2.7 miles. The trail continues just east and south of the River Bend Overlook (south of the park road) and takes users back to the parking area over the course of 1.4 miles.

Buckhorn Trail

Distance: 11.4-mile loop

Finding the trailhead: The Buckhorn Trail can be accessed from numerous locations in the North Unit. The first place to reach the trail is on the right side of the North Unit road, only about 1.2 miles after entering the park. The next easiest access point is at the Cannonball Concretions Pullout, about 3.4 miles farther down the park road.

The hike: The Buckhorn Trail travels through the eastern areas of the North Unit and showcases the beautiful scenery of the Badlands. The trail can be joined from numerous points, making it possible to do just a portion of the trail. It passes through one of the North Unit's prairie dog towns and near the northern boundary of another. It is flat for most of its distance.

Achenbach Trail

Distance: 17.7-mile loop

Finding the trailhead: The Achenbach Trail can be accessed from numerous locations along the North Unit's roads, including Juniper Campground, the Caprock Coulee trailhead, the River Bend Overlook, and the Oxbow Overlook. If you want simple access, start from the Oxbow Overlook, at the end of the park road (13.7 miles straight down the road from the park entrance).

The hike: The Achenbach Trail is like a sister trail to the Buckhorn but is also its opposite in many ways. It travels through the western areas of the North Unit and is much more challenging than the Buckhorn. It also goes through a large portion of the North Unit's wilderness areas, making it very popular among backpackers. The trail has more ups and downs (rather than being a primarily flat trail) and also requires crossing the Little Missouri River at several points. Before heading out, you will need to find out if the river is safe to cross. The trail can be joined at various places and can also be combined with the Buckhorn Trail to make a loop that circles the entire North Unit.

Other Recreation Possibilities in the Park

While bicycling, boating, fishing, and winter activities are logistically more challenging than other activities at Theodore Roosevelt National Park, they can also bring you terrific experiences. Bicycling, in particular, is an activity that I think will grow in popularity in and around the park over the next few years. While fishing is something you *can* do in the park, the Little Missouri River does not offer the premier fishing that North Dakota and nearby areas are known for. In this chapter I have also included a short section on photography.

Bicycling

You cannot bike on any of the trails in Theodore Roosevelt National Park, but it has always surprised me that more people do not choose to bike on the roads. With its pleasant scenery, wildlife, and varying topography (flat areas, gradual uphills, gradual downhills, curves, and straight stretches), the 36-mile scenic loop drive in the South Unit is particularly appealing. The 14-mile North Unit road also makes for a nice bike ride, and it is much more consistently flat. It does, however, have what is probably the most intense uphill/downhill slope within the park. If you choose to ride the roads, make sure that you keep your eyes open for cars. There is usually enough space for them to get by easily, but always be cautious.

If you are interested more in mountain biking than road biking, consider the sections of the Maah Daah Hey Trail outside the park. (See Nearby Excursions and Recreation Opportunities.) If you want to rent a bicycle or take a guided trip, Dakota Cyclery Mountain Bike Adventures (275 Third Avenue West) in Medora is currently the only place to go. The cyclery is open from late May through early October. In addition to renting bikes and guiding trips, Dakota Cyclery also repairs bikes, sells gear, offers shuttle service, and will assemble your bike if you want to ship it to them. For more information call (701) 623–4808 or (888) 321–1218, visit www.dakota cyclery.com, or e-mail sales@dakotacyclery.com.

Boating

If you are looking for white water on the Little Missouri River, you will not find it. The river is a slow, calm float—and that's only when the water is high enough. While a float down the Little Missouri River is definitely not one of the storied journeys that people who canoe and kayak romanticize, it can still be a fun and interesting activity. Theodore Roosevelt had one of his most famous adventures on the river, and on some stretches you will be making the same trip he did. I have been lucky enough to canoe on the river twice. On one of these occasions I watched six beavers as they collected woody material for their dams. The riverbanks are also common places for many other animals to visit, so making a trip down the river is a potential opportunity for superb wildlife viewing. The problem is, in many years the Little Missouri does not reach the necessary depth to make canoeing or kayaking possible. May and June have traditionally been the times when canoeing or kayaking is possible.

If you're thinking of taking a float down the river, here's what you need to know:

- Always check current river conditions ahead of time by calling the park at (701) 623–4466. You can also check the river's depth online at www .waterdata.usgs.gov/nd/nwis.
- If you don't have a canoe or kayak, canoes can be rented from Little Knife Outfitters. (701–842–2631; www.littleknifeoutfitters.com). They also offer shuttle service.

- If you want to travel from the South Unit to the North Unit, it takes three to four days to canoe from Medora to the Long X Bridge on U.S Highway 85.
- When boating, you will likely have to get out and drag your vessel at some point or portage for a short distance. Be prepared.
- Plan on bringing all your own drinking water. There are no sources of potable water available along the river.
- Open fires are not allowed on park lands, so plan on bringing a camp stove for cooking.
- If you plan on camping on an overnight trip within the park, you must get a backcountry permit from one of the park's visitor centers. Much of the land on the journey from the South Unit to the North Unit also borders private land. Use the USFS National Grasslands map to find out where private lands are, and contact the owners of the land in advance for permission to camp on their land.
- Wildlife barriers and electric fences may block your path at several points. You will need to portage around these obstacles.
- If you plan on leaving your vehicle(s) while you're on the river, let park staff know so that they can direct you to the best places to put them.

Little Missouri River Mileages

Information provided courtesy of Theodore Roosevelt National Park.

Mileages, Little Missouri River, South to North

Marmath to Billings County Line	79.0 miles
Billings County Line to Medora	41.5 miles
Medora to Elkhorn Ranch	39.5 miles
Elkhorn Ranch to McKenzie County Line	9.5 miles
McKenzie County Line to US 85 bridge	58.5 miles
US 85 bridge to Highway 22 bridge	40.5 miles
Through South Unit of TR National Park	11.0 miles
Through North Unit of TR National Park	14.5 miles

Fishing

As noted in this chapter's introduction, fishing is not one of the activities that Theodore Roosevelt National Park is known for. But if you have the desire, you can fish the park's only major body of water, the Little Missouri River. Species of fish that live in this murky river include carpsuckers, chubs, catfish, goldeyes, minnows, redhorses, and saugers. Occasionally some other species are around, too. If you want to fish, you will need a North Dakota fishing license and will need to follow the state's fishing regulations. Fishing licenses can be purchased in Medora at the Billings County Courthouse (which is closed on the weekend), in Belfield at the Tesoro Station (open twenty-four hours a day), or in Watford City at the One Stop Station on US 85.

Winter Recreation

If you come to the park in winter, it is quite possible that you might not see the heaps of snow you might expect. Contrary to popular belief, North Dakota does not get an extreme amount of snow. The average winter snowfall is about 30 inches. For comparison, the state of Minnesota gets 35 to 70 inches each year. In the words of several park staff members, "The same snow blows around all winter." But when there is a consistent blanket of snow, the park can make for a fun place to cross-country ski or snowshoe (you will need to bring your own equipment).

According to former South Unit naturalist Victoria Mates, "Within the boundary of Theodore Roosevelt National Park, when conditions permit, the Little Missouri River is the best spot for cross-country skiing. Once the river is frozen and covered with a blanket of snow, skiing through this river valley affords beautiful views of the badlands and opportunities for winter wildlife watching." None of the park trails are groomed for skiing, and thus make for a more challenging, higher risk experience. Snowshoeing only requires snow and that you have the right gear. The topography of the badlands and varying weather conditions might make for snow that has inconsistent depth. As with any time of year, if you take a winter trip into the park's backcountry, be safe. Go with others, and tell people where you are going and when you will be back. Winter can be a great time for wildlife viewing in the park, so have fun.

Photography

You can get some great photographs when visiting Theodore Roosevelt National Park. With or without patience, you can get excellent shots of wildlife, plants, and scenery. Most of the overlooks in the park provide good places for taking photographs, but for those of you who like unique pictures, hike up or around any of the park's buttes to get them. There are not many tall trees in the park, and as cloud cover varies, lighting for taking photos generally ranges from average to superb.

One thing to consider if you go into the backcountry with a camera is bentonitic clay. I tend to carry my camera while walking so that I can quickly take pictures of animals when I see them. You will inevitably cross some stretches where there is a lot of clay, so be careful that the clay does not kick up from your heels (or someone else's) onto your camera. It can be hard to clean. Trust me.

Getting pictures of bison should not be hard. They are often near the road, and you might be able to take photographs right out of your vehicle's window. Make sure that you keep a safe distance from bison (and all wildlife for that matter). The park recommends maintaining a distance of at least 100 yards from bison. A digital or 35mm camera with a zoom will get you pictures of prairie dogs you will like. A tripod-mounted camera with a powerful lens will make the pictures even better. You will need a fast shutter and film speed if you want to get the prairie dogs doing their famous "jump-yip" call. Even if you have the right equipment, getting the timing right for capturing a snapshot of this unique behavior requires patience and can be frustrating.

Coyotes come near the roads more often than you might think. What seems to be *the* key tip about coyotes is to be alert for their presence. If you get into the practice of always scanning the boundaries and interiors of prairie dog towns when you first reach them, you will probably see coyotes and learn more about where they hang out. Waiting patiently at a prairie dog town for about thirty minutes usually does the trick, too.

Once you find wild horses, you should not have trouble getting photographs. Like bison, they usually are not too concerned with your presence, but you also should not approach them. You will probably see a lot of deer, but elk can be more of a challenge to see and photograph. They are wary of people most of the time and will often run up high onto nearby buttes if alarmed. Want to get pronghorn pictures? Good luck! Your best bet is to take a walk around the flat areas near the eastern boundary of the South Unit while being very quiet and having a powerful lens on your camera that you can hold steady.

The park is also an excellent place for getting porcupine photographs. That's right! Porcupine photographs. If you drive on the park roads right before sunset, it is very likely that you will see porcupines. Getting the right focus is key for getting a good porcupine photograph. With all of those quills, they are a challenge. You'll see what I mean. If you are a birder, try the campgrounds or spots near the Little Missouri River.

Here's my concluding point about photography in the park: Make sure that when you take photographs you stay safe and keep a safe distance from all animals—bison most of all. You want to see those pictures some day, don't you?

Other National Park Service Sites in North Dakota

There are a total of three National Park Service sites in North Dakota. Although Knife River Indian Villages National Historic Site and Fort Union Trading Post National Historic Site are not as well known as Theodore Roosevelt National Park, both are well worth visiting. They relate to a subject that Theodore Roosevelt National Park does not cover in great detail: American Indians and their history on the Northern Plains and the fur trade on the Upper Missouri River. From Medora, it's about two to two and a half hours to each site.

Knife River Indian Villages National Historic Site

It is a satisfying feeling to look out onto a preserved landscape and know that what you see today is similar, if not the same, to what people saw in the distant past. At Knife River Indian Villages, the opposite is true. You can stand at this National Park Service site—with its relative quiet, peacefulness, and plain landscape—and know that what you see and feel today is probably in utter contrast to the sounds, activity, and landscape that would have been part of a thriving community that was here just about 200 years ago.

Several groups of Hidatsa and Mandan peoples once called Knife River their home. They lived here in homes called earthlodges and relied upon agriculture as the cornerstone of their way of life. The Knife River area provided fish and other resources, making it an attractive place to live, an exciting place to visit, and an enticing place for other tribes to attack. The rampant spread of smallpox in 1837 drastically reduced the populations of the Hidatsa and Mandan as well as other native peoples across the United States. The disease's destructive powers prompted people to move away from Knife River to the west and north. With decimated populations, the Hidatsa and Mandan were soon joined by the Arikara, a former enemy, for the protection and comfort of increased numbers. There are now only a few visible signs of the thriving civilization that once existed at Knife River.

The Mandan, Hidatsa, and Arikara nations are now collectively known as the "Three Affiliated Tribes." Their primary home today is the Fort Berthold Reservation, located to the northwest of the Knife River. The historic site at Knife River Indian Villages provides you with an opportunity to learn more about these people, hear stories about how they lived, and ponder the powerful history of one of their former communities.

Basic Park Information

Where is the park? It is located just north of Stanton, North Dakota.

When can I go? The site is open daily, with some holidays excluded. Visitor facilities operate on mountain time from 8:00 A.M. to 4:30 P.M., with expanded hours in summer.

How much does it cost? There is no admission charge.

How much time will I need? Allow at least one and one-half to two hours.

What if I'm hungry? If you plan on eating before or after your visit to Knife River, there are a couple options. For those who choose to bring their own food, a sheltered picnic area is available. If you want to purchase a meal, the closest places are just to the south in the very small town of Stanton or about 9 miles to the west in the larger community of Hazen.

Where can I stay? Accommodations and camping are available in many of the nearby communities.

Can I take my pet? Pets are allowed on the trails but must always be on a leash. They are not allowed in the buildings.

Resources: For in-depth, up-to-date information, check the park's Web site (www.nps.gov/knri), or call (701) 745–3300 to speak to a park staff member.

The reconstructed earthlodge behind the visitor center provides an excellent idea of what homes were like for people at Knife River.

Touring Knife River Indian Villages

When you arrive at Knife River, be sure to take notice of the exterior design of the visitor center building. Inside the visitor center you will find exhibits, a Theodore Roosevelt Nature & History Association bookstore, an information desk, and restrooms. You can also watch a fifteen-minute film about the people of Knife River and their culture. If you have children, ask for one of the fun and educational Junior Ranger booklets.

Next walk through the back door of the visitor center. A round-trip walk of about 1.25 miles will allow you to see a reconstructed earthlodge, two of the historic village sites, and the Knife River. Interpretive signs along the path provide information of interest. For instance, you can read more about Hidatsa fishing techniques, the types of plants the people of Knife River grew, and archaeology efforts at the site. With some assistance, the flat trail is accessible to people using wheelchairs (part of the trail is gravel).

In summer, park staff members offer hourly talks inside the reconstructed earthlodge. Its furnishings are interesting and will paint a vivid picture in your mind of what life was like inside these cozy dwellings. Be sure to notice how a corral was used to protect the most prized horses from weather and theft. Also note the clever use of suspended vertical storage containers known as parfleche. Does the earthlodge feel spacious to you? About ten to twenty persons would typically live in one of these structures.

Walking a little farther down the path, you will next come to the Lower Hidatsa Village Site. Take a few moments to walk out and across the depressions you see in the ground. Dorothy Cook, Knife River's interpretive specialist, explains, "When you look at the depressions after having seen the reconstructed earthlodge, you can visualize how the people lived. You can use your senses and hear the kids playing. You can smell the meals cooking."

We know a lot about the culture of the people who lived at Knife River thanks to information, stories, and history provided by the tribes. In addition, countless artifacts, works of art, historical writings (from people like Lewis and Clark), and archaeological studies help us understand the lives of these people. The Hidatsa and Mandan shared many aspects of what we refer to as Plains Indian culture. Of course, each tribe also had cultural differences that made it unique. Intermarriage between the Hidatsa and Mandan made the specific cultures of these two groups less distinctive at Knife River, and the cultures soon became very hard to tell apart. As previously mentioned, agriculture provided ample sustenance for these people so that they did not have to move very often. It was a matriarchal society, where women built and owned the earthlodges, tended the gardens, and took care of most domestic affairs. When a man married a woman, he came and lived with her family. The primary role of men was to hunt bison and other animals, protect the villages, and sometimes to make war on other tribes. Trade, games, and ceremonies also were a big part of life here. While visiting the site, you can understand the culture of these people in greater detail by reading the materials the park offers, viewing the exhibits, and talking to park staff members.

Continuing on, there is a longer stretch of walking to do between the Lower Hidatsa Village Site and the Sakakawea Site. As I walked, I personally found that the tranquil setting and light rustle of the wind through the grass created a mood perfect for contemplation. It is amazing to think about how quickly people can come and go. What lasting artifacts will we leave behind as people and communities? As time marches on, what will people find to be of importance or interest about our own cultures?

You will soon reach the Sakakawea Village Site, a place named for the woman who would serve as the Lewis and Clark Expedition's most famous guide. She was living at this village on the Knife River when Lewis and Clark met her. To quote Dorothy Cook again, "When you walk out to the village sites or walk the trail you can ask yourself, 'Is this where Lewis and Clark walked? Is this where Sakakawea walked?' To me, other than Civil War sites, there are not many National Park Service sites where you can truly say of people from history, 'I may be walking in their footsteps.'"

After seeing the Sakakawea Village Site, continue on the path and walk down a set of stairs that lead to the Knife River. Follow the path to your right and you will have completed a short loop back to the Lower Hidatsa Site. Upon returning to the visitor center, take another look at the inside of the building. Is there anything you did not notice before? Is there something familiar about the pillars?

Additional Things to Do at Knife River

If you want to see and do more at Knife River than what is described above—you can.

Another village site, known as the Big Hidatsa Site, can be viewed by driving a few miles north of the visitor center, parking, and then walking. In addition, there are about 15 miles of trails you can walk at Knife River. In winter you can cross-country ski on some of these trails if there is enough snow and if the conditions are right. You can also fish at Knife River or enjoy some bird-watching. The park offers special educational programs and events throughout the year. For instance, the Northern Plains Indian Culture Fest is held annually on the last full weekend of July. Check the Web site listed above for more information about when these events occur.

Fort Union Trading Post National Historic Site

From 1828 to 1867 Fort Union was one of the major centers of trade between American Indians and white entrepreneurs in the American West. With the approval of a tribe known as the Assiniboin, the American Fur Company built Fort Union as a trading post in Assiniboin territory near the confluence of the Missouri and Yellowstone Rivers. The Assiniboin became the primary people who traded for goods at Fort Union, and they came to view themselves as the protectors of the trading post and its inhabitants. The fort's excellent location helped encourage other tribes to come to Fort Union to trade, including the Crow, Blackfeet, Cree, Hidatsa, Lakota, and Metis.

Loren Yellow Bird is a park ranger at Fort Union Trading Post and is also a member of the Arikara Nation. Yellow Bird explains that Fort Union is significant because it represents "a connection between the cultures of white traders and the American Indians who came here to trade. It was the union of two cultures. In these connections, there are a world of stories that depict the good, bad, and changes that were part of the trading post's history, as well as the history of the American West." At least six American Indian languages and ten European languages were spoken within the walls of Fort Union at one time or another. The whites who worked for the fort came from numerous countries and often married American Indian women. As a result, a large portion of people who lived in and around Fort Union were of mixed heritage, strengthening the bonds between cultures.

Many famous people of the frontier period visited Fort Union over the years, including Sitting Bull, Jim Bridger, George Catlin, and John James Audubon. Visitors and employees of the fort created written accounts, as well as paintings and drawings that illuminate the fort's colorful history.

In 1837 and 1857 smallpox epidemics decimated American Indian populations near Fort Union and across the West. Disease in combination with growing hostilities between the U.S. government and western tribes helped contribute to the decline of Fort Union. Around 1866 the American Fur Company sold the trading post to the Northwest Fur Company, which sold the trading post to the U.S. Army in 1867. The army took the trading post apart to obtain materials to finish the construction of a new military installation—Fort Buford, only 3 miles away.

When Fort Union was excavated by the National Park Service in the 1960s, countless artifacts from the past were found. Today the historic site possesses one of the most extensive archaeological collections in the National Park Service, with more than 1.6 million artifacts. The vast amount of artifacts, journals, and artwork left behind helped the National Park Service build an accurate reconstruction of Fort Union. The fort that you now see was built over the course of seven years, starting in 1985. The reconstructed fort was placed right on top of the foundations of the historic fort.

A visit to Fort Union Trading Post National Historic Site today will allow you to learn more about the role of trade between American Indians and whites in the American West. You can learn more about Fort Union's significance and ponder how this place helped to forge friendships and facilitate the sharing of cultures.

Basic Park Information

Where is the park? Fort Union is located on the Montana–North Dakota border, southwest of Williston, North Dakota.

When can I go? The site is open daily, with some holidays excluded. Visitor facilities operate on central time from 9:00 A.M. to 5:30 P.M., with expanded hours in summer (currently 8:00 A.M. to 8:00 P.M.).

How much does it cost? There is no admission charge.

How much time will I need? Allow at least one to two hours.

What if I'm hungry? If you plan on eating before or after your visit to Fort Union, there are a couple options. If you bring your own food, there are places to picnic around the fort's grounds. If you want to purchase a meal, the closest places are Fairview, Montana, to the south and Williston, North Dakota, to the east.

Where can I stay? Accommodations and camping are available in many of the nearby communities.

Can I take my pet? Pets are not allowed in the buildings. They are allowed on the grounds with a leash.

Resources: For in-depth, up-to-date information, check the park's Web site (www.nps.gov/fous), or call (701) 572–9083 to speak to a park staff member.

Touring Fort Union Trading Post

When you arrive at Fort Union, notice how the design of the fort creates a sense of mystery that makes you want to know what's inside. Do you think this design was intentional or simply for defense? Before walking inside, notice the painting above the fort's main gate. It symbolizes how the fort was a place where two cultures came together, as earlier described by Loren Yellow Bird.

Once inside the fort, the large house ahead of you is where the site's visitor center is located. It's called the Bourgeois House. Historically this building was where the bourgeois (or manager) of the fort lived in addition to his most important aides. A bold man named Kenneth McKenzie was the trading post's first bourgeois. McKenzie set a high standard that his successors would attempt to emulate, and he is credited for much of the fort's success. Today the Bourgeois House serves as the visitor center for Fort Union as well as an office for park staff members. Inside you will find exhibits, restrooms, and a bookstore run by the Fort Union Association that

Fort Union Trading Post was a rarity during our nation's frontier period: For nearly forty years it was a place where American Indians and whites peacefully exchanged their goods and cultures.

carries an extensive variety of books about Fort Union, American Indians, and the American West. If you have kids, be sure to ask for one of the Junior Trader programs (a clever variation of the Junior Ranger program). Once you have gathered your bearings and information about the site, head back outside to the fort.

There are quite a few interpretive signs to read and places to see within Fort Union. One of the places you will definitely want to see is the Trade House. The Trade House was the center of activity at Fort Union. In summer this part of the fort is staffed by people who do living history. They will tell you more about what life was like at Fort Union, the items that people traded, and the rituals associated with trading at the fort.

The Trade House had three rooms. The Reception Room was where one first entered the trading post and was where most of the trading took place. Indians who visited the trading post were usually invited to eat and sit near a warm fireplace before any talk of trading occurred. Next the on-duty trader would offer his guests tobacco and make a brief speech that highlighted the peace and friendship of the trading post with the visiting tribe. A chief of the visiting tribe would, in turn, reiterate the points of the trader in a speech. Once this custom was honored, some gifts might be exchanged, and the process of setting prices for goods began. Usually Indians brought buffalo robes or furs to sell. Negotiations might take hours. When the value of goods was agreed upon, trading would commence.

Adjacent to the Reception Room was the Trading Shop. In this room a variety of up to 250 items were stocked for a customer's perusal. Some of these items included weapons, tin cups, cloth, beads, and tools. Today you can see replica items in the Trading Shop and understand how this "store" would have been an exciting place for people to visit.

To supplement its food supplies, the trading post hired hunters to bring fresh meat to the table. They would also trade with Indians for food. Loren Yellow Bird notes that "the trading post would from time to time trade with some of the village tribes that were more sedentary, like the Mandan and Arikara. They would be trading their items for corn, squash, and beans, as this would help the fort have food longer than their supplies would have allowed them."

The final room you will want to see in the Trading House is the Clerk's Office. This area was essentially a clerical office. At times, however, it was transformed into a meeting space for Indian chiefs and the current bourgeois of the trading post.

While at the fort, take time to walk up to the Southwest and Northeast Bastions. The bastions were the fort's primary fixtures for defense. Up top you can see how these positions offer commanding views of the areas surrounding the fort. While there were a few moments of high tension between American Indians and the traders of Fort Union, serious conflicts were averted. The bastions ended up serving as more of a symbolic show of power than as a necessary method of protection.

There is one other object of interest I recommend not missing. You might have noticed the Buffalo Robe Press right outside the fort's main entrance. This interesting device would be used to press ten buffalo robes at a time into a bundle. Bundles were then shipped via boat downriver, where they would be sold to eager eastern buyers.

Special Events At Fort Union

Fort Union hosts several annual events that draw crowds and offer opportunities for visitors to have enhanced experiences. Every June the trading post has its largest special event, known as the Fort Union Rendezvous. This event takes place in honor of the rendezvous of old and is essentially a large gathering with speakers, reenactors, demonstrations, and people selling the types of furs and crafts you could have found during the Fort Union period. The rendezvous usually takes place during the third weekend of June, Father's Day weekend.

Every August the historic site offers an Indian Arts Showcase. This event typically occurs during the first weekend of August. Demonstrations and programs highlight various aspects of traditional and modern American Indian cultures. Crafts are also sold.

The summer season wraps up with the Labor Day Living History Weekend. The historic site likes to note that this event is the most accurate depiction of what life was like at Fort Union Trading Post. On this weekend more than the typical offerings of programs are presented by park staff in historical dress as period characters.

One other event that the park recommends takes place at Fort Buford, a military post rather than a trading post. The Fort Buford Military Encampment depicts life for soldiers at the fort in the 1870s.

Nearby Excursions and Recreation Opportunities

Picking places to mention in this chapter required hours and hours of research and personal visits. Just about every little town in North Dakota seems to have its own museum. I've tried to do the work for you and mention the places that I think represent the best that the western regions of North Dakota offer based on my own experiences and the recommendations of others.

The Maah Daah Hey Trail

The Maah Daah Hey Trail has become a popular destination for recreation seekers. The name in Mandan means "an area that has been or will be around for a long time." This National Recreation Trail is a hiking, mountain biking, and horseback riding trail that stretches 96 miles and connects all three units of Theodore Roosevelt National Park. The trail goes through areas of private land, state land, the Little Missouri National Grasslands (701–225–5151; www.fs.fed.us/r1/dakotaprairie/mdhtl.htm) and the South and North Units of Theodore Roosevelt National Park (701–623–4466; www.nps.gov/thro/tr_mdh.htm). It is managed by the USDA

Forest Service and also the National Park Service. The trail allows for appreciation of the scenic badlands wildlife and also passes by the Ice Caves (www.state.nd.us/ndgs/caves/caves_h.htm). These caves received their name from the ice that forms indefinitely on the cave's floors and are accessed by a short trail from the Maah Daah Hey.

The Maah Daah Hey is numbered starting from Sully Creek State Park and connects that site to the CCC campground just south of the North Unit. A turtle symbol is used for trail markers. Six campgrounds are located along the route, and in summer the campgrounds have the potable water that you need to travel safely, as well as campfire rings and vault toilets. Bicycles cannot be used or carried on the trail in Theodore Roosevelt National Park, and for this reason the Buffalo Gap Trail was created. It is a 22-mile spur that starts at Sully Creek State Park Campground and bypasses the South Unit. It uses a bison skull symbol for trail markers.

Weather can affect the trail just like all other trails in the Badlands, making it impassable if very wet. Several lodges offer guided trips of the trail, lodging, and shuttle services. More information can be found online, as well as by contacting the National Park Service or the USDA Forest Service.

Places of Interest North of the Park

About an hour north of the North Unit, you will find Lake Sakakawea. This large lake is one of North Dakota's recreation jewels. The Web site for Lake Sakakawea State Park (www.parkrec.nd.gov/Parks/LSSP.htm) claims that the 368,000-acre lake, which connects to the Missouri River, is "one of the three largest man-made reservoirs in the nation." The state park (701–487–3315) is located on the southern side of the lake. Countless other places to stay and camp, including Lewis and Clark State Park (701–859–3071), blanket the lake's surroundings. As you might guess, fishing is one of the popular activities on the lake. You can catch a variety of fish, including chinook salmon, walleye, and several other species. Other water recreation activities are also popular, including windsurfing.

Surrounding most of Lake Sakakawea is the Fort Berthold Reservation, which is home to the Arikara, Mandan, and Hidatsa Nations. On the northern border of the reservation, in New Town, you will find the Three Affiliated Tribes Museum (701–627–4477; www.mhanation.com). The museum has exhibits about the tribes and their history.

In addition to Fort Union Trading Post National Historic Site (discussed in the previous chapter), Fort Buford (701–572–9034; www.state.nd

.us/hist/buford/buford.htm) is a place you may want to visit. This military post was an important place for the U.S. Army and was the location where the Sioux chief Sitting Bull eventually surrendered in 1881. There are several original buildings remaining and a museum. A few minutes away is the Missouri-Yellowstone Confluence Interpretive Center (701–572–9034; www.state.nd.us/hist/lewisclark/attractions_mycic.html). The fort is open daily in summer and by appointment at other times of the year.

Places of Interest East of the Park

The city of Dickinson (www.dickinsonnd.com) is about forty minutes east of Medora. The closest city of significant size to the park, Dickinson has a population of about 17,000 and is home to Dickinson State University. You can access a lot of stores, restaurants, and services in the city.

One place that might be of interest to you in Dickinson is the Dakota Dinosaur Museum (701–225–3466; www.dakotadino.com). The museum boasts eleven full-scale dinosaurs as well as countless other paleontological and geological specimens. It is open May through Labor Day from 9:00 A.M. to 5:00 P.M.

About 20 miles east of Dickinson, on Interstate 94 at exit 72, you will see what the *Guinness Book of World Records* lists as the largest scrap metal sculpture in the world. *Geese in Flight* is 110 feet tall and 154 feet wide. It cost more than $150,000 to make and was created by artist Gary Greff. If you like this sculpture, the good news is that there are more nearby. Greff has made six other sculptures that are spaced along what has become known as the Enchanted Highway (701–563–6400; www.enchantedhighway.net). To see the other sculptures on the Enchanted Highway, drive south from exit 72 on County Road 4531. In 32 miles you will reach the town of Regent, where the Enchanted Highway concludes with a gift shop.

About two hours east of Medora on I–94 you will come to the city of Mandan, home to Fort Abraham Lincoln State Park (701–667–6340; www.parkrec.nd.gov/Parks/FLSP.htm). This park has a beautiful campground along the Heart River and a wealth of history to discover. The area was occupied by Mandan Indians for a period ranging from about 1575 to 1781. The park has reconstructed a set of earthlodges, collectively known as the "On-A-Slant-Village," to help interpret Mandan life. Several forts were later built at this location, and the later fort has the distinction of being where General Custer was stationed with his unit of cavalry before marching to his fatal fight with several tribes at the Battle of Little Bighorn.

The Tin Family, *one of the largest scrap metal sculptures in the world, is located along the "Enchanted Highway" with six other large sculptures.*

Various parts of the fort, as well as Custer's house, have been reconstructed. A visitor center provides exhibits about the fort's history, and tours are offered. The park is open year-round, although the visitor center, fort, and On-A-Slant-Village are only open in summer.

Just 4 miles east of Mandan is Bismarck (www.bismarck.org), North Dakota's capital city. Bismarck is a large city with a population of about 55,000. In 2005 the Dakota Zoo (701–223–7543; www.dakotazoo.org) was voted the best city attraction by readers of the *Bismarck Tribune*. It has a surprising array of animals, totaling more than 125 species. The zoo is open all year, with extended hours in summer.

About 40 miles north of Bismarck, near the town of Washburn, the Lewis and Clark expedition stayed with the Mandan and Hidatsa near Knife River during the winter of 1804–1805. The expedition built cabins in an enclosure that came to be known as Fort Mandan. The reconstructed fort and the North Dakota Lewis and Clark Interpretive Center (which are very close to Knife River Indian Villages National Historic Site) interpret the role of the Lewis and Clark expedition in North Dakota. The fort and center are open all year from 9:00 A.M. to 5:00 P.M., with extended summer hours.

A final place to mention is Killdeer Mountain Battlefield State Historic Site. An 1864 battle was fought here between the Sioux and U.S. Army forces commanded by General Alfred Sully. A small interpretive sign explains the battle. The battlefield is located about 10 miles northwest of the town of Killdeer.

Places of Interest South of the Park

To the south of Medora there are numerous museums and the tourist attraction–laden Black Hills area. I will note two places. One is White Butte (3,506 feet), the highest point in North Dakota. The other is the intriguing Fort Dilts State Historic Site. A wagon train of settlers bound for Montana and some soldiers serving as escorts were attacked here in 1864 by a band of the Lakota. The party erected a sod fort 6 feet high and 2 feet thick, which shielded them for fourteen days until they were rescued by a troop of soldiers. The fort is not standing today, but a small monument marks its location.

Places of Interest West of the Park

You really aren't far from Montana when you're at Theodore Roosevelt National Park. The state has many interesting places to visit, and a thorough discussion of what you can see and do there is beyond the scope of this book. One place I will suggest is Makoshika State Park (406–365–6256) located near the city of Glendive (about an hour west on I–94 from Medora). This park contains 11,531 acres of badlands, with a campground, several trails, a dinosaur display, and plenty of wildlife. To the west in Montana are also the tourist juggernauts of Yellowstone and Glacier National Parks, and Little Bighorn Battlefield National Monument.

Fishing and Hunting

North Dakota is known for its great fishing and hunting. Aside from Lake Sakakawea to the north, other options within an hour or two of Theodore Roosevelt National Park include smaller bodies of water like Camel Hump Lake, Buffalo Gap Dam, Sather Dam, and Belfield Pond. These fishing

A group of settlers traveling to Montana were attacked by a band of the Lakota and erected a small sod fort (Fort Dilts) for their defense.

holes contain a variety of fish, including pike, trout, bluegill, and bass. North Dakota fishing licenses are required for any fishing you do.

Where there's a lot of wildlife, there's also a lot of hunting. Many of the accommodations listed in this book offer hunting packages or options. North Dakota is known for great duck, goose, pheasant, grouse, deer, antelope, and elk hunting. For more information about fishing, hunting, and licenses, visit www.ndtourism.com. Also check the list of hunting guides listed below.

Hunting Guides

Badlands Elk Ranch (62 125th Avenue NW) offers guided elk hunting on private ranch. For rates and information visit www.badlandshunt.com, call (701) 863-6722, or e-mail: info@badlandshunt.com.

Badlands Guide Service offers numerous guided hunting experiences in and around the Badlands. For rates and information visit www

.badlandsguideservice.com, call (701) 225–6109, or e-mail: badlands@ndsupernet.com.

Dakota Adventures Outfitter and Guide Services offers guided hunting trips. For rates and information call (701) 842–3415 or e-mail gadefoe@ruggedwest.com.

Deep Creek Adventures offers guided hunting and ATV trips. For rates and information visit www.deepcreekadventures.com, call (701) 759–3460, or e-mail: BarURanch@deepcreekadventures.com.

You and the Future of Theodore Roosevelt National Park

After you have visited the park, you will know why Theodore Roosevelt National Park sings to the hearts of its visitors. One of the things I like so much about the park is how it represents the kinds of parks and protected areas I think we will probably have more of in the future. It's relatively small, split into units, and adjacent to communities of people. The park reminds us of how people and nature can coexist, even if in relatively small spaces.

Philosophically and practically, I personally believe that we as people are not separate from nature but part of it. In the park we get the chance to see how Theodore Roosevelt's relationship and interactions with nature in the badlands of western Dakota Territory inspired him to help conserve the natural resources of his country. While we should appreciate him for such heroic acts, it is a disservice to ourselves if we are always waiting for such a hero to achieve what we want for our future. We as individuals have the power to make changes in the world, but only if we choose to use that

power. As Roosevelt understood, our human needs demand the use of some natural resources. He also understood that we must take care to make sure that those resources last. I hope that you strive to follow his example whenever it is practical for you to do so and also take care to tell others about the wonderful park that bears his name. I'm sure he would appreciate it.

Appendix A
Additional Resources

Rather than simply giving you a list of books and Web sites, I thought I would provide you with a bit of commentary. Take from it what you will. The park's bookstores sell many of the books I discuss, and a list can be found online at www.nps.gov/thro/tr_shop.htm. These bookstores are operated by the Theodore Roosevelt Nature & History Association—a non-profit group that donates a major portion of its profits to park projects and programs.

Theodore Roosevelt

I have found more than twenty biographies of Theodore Roosevelt in libraries and online. Each author makes his or her own stance on some aspect of Roosevelt's life or presidency. The most straightforward, chronological biography I have found is Nathan Miller's *Theodore Roosevelt: A Life*. Just about any biography seems to have its strengths, though. I've looked at few that were bad or boring to read.

The history that we have of Roosevelt in the West is based on some facts and probably some fiction—or romanticized versions of truth. One of the best sources of information and stories is Hermann Hagedorn's fun-to-read book, *Roosevelt in the Badlands*. Much of the information Hagedorn provides came from firsthand accounts supplied by Roosevelt and his contemporaries—making the accuracy of some of the stories in the book suspect but very rich and lively in their detail. Another good source is a fifty-one-page pamphlet published by the National Park Service with a similar title, *Theodore Roosevelt and the Dakota Badlands*. And of course, Theodore Roosevelt's own writings provide firsthand accounts of his experiences in North Dakota and elsewhere.

The best online source for information about Theodore Roosevelt is the Theodore Roosevelt Association Web site (www.theodoreroosevelt.org). It's fantastic.

I also want to mention one of the best books I've ever found about U.S. presidents: *To the Best of My Ability: The American Presidents*. I found it while visiting Jimmy Carter National Historic Site. Each president is succinctly covered in about four to six pages, with great photographs and interesting details. The book's entries are a great resource and are written by many of the top historians of our time.

Theodore Roosevelt National Park

The place to start if you want to learn more about the park is by asking park staff members questions or by attending interpretive programs. If those options aren't possible, or you'd rather learn on your own, then the standard park brochure, park newspaper, and Web site (www.nps.gov/thro) are full of information and good places to begin. I also suggest *The Roadlog Guide to Theodore Roosevelt National Park* or the popular *Theodore Roosevelt National Park: the Story Behind the Scenery.*

Native Americans

There are numerous books about Native Americans. Some focus on tribes that share cultural traits, while others talk about one tribe. I have read a lot of books about Native Americans, but few of those have specifically covered the tribes of North Dakota. One of the few books that comes to mind is Stephen Ambrose's Lewis and Clark chronicle, *Undaunted Courage.* I seem to recall that it discusses the Mandan and Hidatsa with detail, but it probably is not the most thorough source. I suggest visiting the Three Affiliated Tribes Web site at www.mhanation.com or browsing other books for more information.

Wildlife

Each year, more and more books come out about wildlife. They seem to be improving all the time. I will make only one suggestion here: Buy the small pamphlet *It's A Prairie Dog's Life* if you want to get more information about prairie dogs. If you Google just about any animal on the Internet, you will get tons of pages of varying quality.

Plants

Wildflowers, Grasses & Other Plants of the Northern Plains and Black Hills always worked well for me when I worked for the park and wanted to identify plants. No one plant guide seems to have it all, though: good illustrations, biological information, and interpretive information. I recommend flipping through the books the park sells and choosing one that you like.

Geology

Did you read the "Park Geology: Non-Drowsy Formula" sidebar? That probably tells you everything you need to know about my recommendations for geology books. Try the *Geologic Story of the Great Plains, The Geology of Theodore Roosevelt National Park,* or *A Roadlog Guide to Theodore Roosevelt National Park.*

Appendix B

National Forests, Monuments, Preserves, and Parks Designated by Theodore Roosevelt

During his presidency Theodore Roosevelt was responsible for conserving an extraordinary amount of land and resources. During his administration 150 national forests, 51 federal bird preserves, 18 national monuments, 5 national parks, and 4 federal wildlife preserves were created. He also initiated numerous conservation conferences and commissions as well as reclamation projects (irrigation projects). *National Geographic* estimates that Roosevelt is directly responsible for helping protect 230 million acres—an impressive amount of land.

Some of the places on the following list have changed in their designations over time and therefore might now have different names from those you see on the list. For example, Mount Olympus National Monument is now Olympic National Park. In addition, some of these locations are no longer preserves or are managed by state governments or other agencies. The dates when these preserves were created are also listed.

This information is provided and kindly reprinted courtesy of The Theodore Roosevelt Association, P.O. Box 719, Oyster Bay, NY 11771; www.theodoreroosevelt.org.

Alaska

Behring (Bering) Sea Bird Preserve	February 27, 1909
Bogoslof Bird Preserve	March 2, 1909
Chugach National Forest	February 23, 1909
Fire Island Wildlife Preserve	February 27, 1909

Pribilof Bird Preserve	February 27, 1909
Saint Lazaria Bird Preserve	February 27, 1909
Tongass National Forest	February 16, 1909
Tuxedni Bird Preserve	February 27, 1909
Yukon Delta Bird Preserve	February 27, 1909

Arkansas

Arkansas National Forest	February 27, 1909

Arizona

Apache National Forest	March 2, 1909
Chiricahua National Forest	July 1, 1908
Coconino National Forest	July 1, 1908
Coronado National Forest	July 1, 1908
Crook National Forest	July 1, 1908
Dixie National Forest	February 10, 1909
Garces National Forest	July 1, 1908
Grand Canyon National Monument	January 11, 1908
Grand Canyon Wildlife Preserve	June 23, 1908
Kaibab National Forest	July 1, 1908
Montezuma Castle National Monument	December 8, 1906
Petrified Forest National Monument	December 8, 1906
Prescott National Forest	February 1, 1909
Salt River Bird Preserve	February 25, 1909
Salt River Reclamation Project	March 14, 1903
Sitgreaves National Forest	March 2, 1909
Tonto National Forest	February 10, 1909

Tonto National Monument	December 19, 1907
Tumacacori National Monument	September 15, 1908
Yuma Reclamation Project	May 10, 1904
Zuni National Forest	March 2, 1909

California

Angeles National Forest	July 1, 1908
Calaveras Bigtree National Forest	February 8, 1909
Cinder Cone National Monument	May 6, 1907
Cleveland National Forest	January 26, 1909
Crater National Forest	July 1, 1908
East Park Bird Preserve	February 25, 1909
Farallon Bird Preserve	February 27, 1909
Inyo National Forest	July 1, 1908
Klamath National Forest	February 13, 1909
Klamath Lake Bird Preserve	August 8, 1908
Klamath Reclamation Project	May 15, 1905
Lassen National Forest	March 2, 1909
Lassen Peak National Monument	May 6, 1907
Modoc National Forest	February 25, 1909
Mono National Forest	March 2, 1909
Monterey National Forest	July 1, 1908
Muir Woods National Monument	January 9, 1908
Orland Reclamation Project	October 5, 1907
Pinnacles National Monument	January 16, 1908
Plumas National Forest	March 2, 1909
San Luis National Forest	July 1, 1908

Santa Barbara National Forest	July 1, 1908
Sequoia National Forest	March 2, 1909
Shasta National Forest	March 2, 1909
Sierra National Forest	July 1, 1908
Stanislaus National Forest	July 1, 1908
Tahoe National Forest	March 2, 1909
Trinity National Forest	March 2, 1909
Yuma Reclamation Project	May 10, 1904

Colorado

Arapaho National Forest	July 1, 1908
Battlement National Forest	July 1, 1908
Cochetopa National Forest	July 1, 1908
Gunnison National Forest	July 1, 1908
Hayden National Forest	July 1, 1908
Holy Cross National Forest	July 1, 1908
Las Animas National Forest	March 1, 1907
Leadville National Forest	July 1, 1908
Montezuma National Forest	July 1, 1908
Medicine Bow National Forest	July 1, 1908
Mesa Verde National Park	June 29, 1906
Montezuma National Forest	July 1, 1908
Pike National Forest	July 1, 1908
Rio Grande National Forest	July 1, 1908
Routt National Forest	July 1, 1908
San Isabel National Forest	July 1, 1908
San Juan National Forest	July 1, 1908

Uncompahgre National Forest	July 1, 1908
Uncompahgre Reclamation Project	March 14, 1903
Wheeler National Monument	December 7, 1908
White River National Forest	May 21, 1904

Florida

Choctawhatchee National Forest	November 27, 1908
Indian Key Bird Preserve	February 10, 1906
Island Bay Bird Preserve	October 23, 1908
Key West Bird Preserve	August 8, 1908
Matlacha Pass Bird Preserve	September 26, 1908
Mosquito Inlet Bird Preserve	February 24, 1908
Ocala National Forest	November 24, 1908
Palma Sola Bird Preserve	September 26, 1908
Passage Key Bird Preserve	October 10, 1905
Pelican Island Bird Preserve	March 14, 1903
Pine Island Bird Preserve	September 15, 1908
Tortugas Keys Bird Preserve	April 6, 1908

Hawaii

Hawaiian Islands Bird Preserve	February 3, 1909

Idaho

Bitterroot National Forest	July 1, 1908
Boise National Forest	July 1, 1908
Boise Reclamation Project	March 27, 1905
Cache National Forest	July 1, 1908

Caribou National Forest	January 15, 1907
Challis National Forest	July 1, 1908
Clearwater National Forest	July 1, 1908
Coeur D'Alene National Forest	July 1, 1908
Deer Flat Bird Preserve	February 25, 1909
Idaho National Forest	July 1, 1908
Kaniksu National Forest	July 1, 1908
Lemhi National Forest	July 1, 1908
Minidoka Bird Preserve	February 25, 1909
Minidoka National Forest	July 1, 1908
Minidoka Reclamation Project	April 23, 1904
Nez Perce National Forest	July 1, 1908
Payette National Forest	July 1, 1908
Pend d'Orielle National Forest	July 1, 1908
Pocatello National Forest	July 1, 1908
Salmon National Forest	July 1, 1908
Sawtooth National Forest	July 1, 1908
Targhee National Forest	July 1, 1908
Weiser National Forest	July 1, 1908

Kansas

Kansas National Forest	May 15, 1908

Louisiana

Breton Island Bird Preserve	October 4, 1904
East Timbalier Island Bird Preserve	December 7, 1907
Shell Keys Bird Preserve	August 17, 1907
Tern Islands Bird Preserve	August 8, 1907

Michigan

Huron Islands Bird Preserve	October 10, 1905
Marquette National Forest	February 10, 1909
Michigan National Forest	February 11, 1909
Siskiwit Islands Bird Preserve	October 10, 1905

Minnesota

Minnesota National Forest	May 23, 1908
Superior National Forest	February 13, 1909

Montana

Absaroka National Forest	July 1, 1908
Beartooth National Forest	July 1, 1908
Beaverhead National Forest	July 1, 1908
Bitterroot National Forest	July 1, 1908
Blackfeet National Forest	July 1, 1908
Blackfeet Reservation Reclamation Project	no date available
Cabinet National Forest	July 1, 1908
Custer National Forest	July 1, 1908
Deerlodge National Forest	July 1, 1908
Flathead National Forest	July 1, 1908
Flathead Reservation Reclamation Project	no date available
Fort Peck Reservation Reclamation Project	no date available
Gallatin National Forest	July 1, 1908
Helena National Forest	July 1, 1908
Huntley Reclamation Project	April 18, 1905
Jefferson National Forest	July 1, 1908

Kootenai National Forest	July 1, 1908
Lower Yellowstone Reclamation Project	May 10, 1904
Milk River Reclamation Project	March 14, 1903
National Bison Range	March 4, 1909
Lewis and Clark National Forest	July 1, 1908
Lewis and Clark National Monument	May 11, 1908
Lolo National Forest	November 6, 1906
Madison National Forest	July 1, 1908
Missoula National Forest	July 1, 1908
Sioux National Forest	February 15, 1909
Sun River Reclamation Project	February 26, 1906
Willow Creek Bird Preserve	February 25, 1909

Nebraska

Nebraska National Forest	July 1, 1908
North Platte Reclamation Project	March 14, 1903

Nevada

Humboldt National Forest	January 20, 1909
Moapa National Forest	January 21, 1909
Mono National Forest	March 2, 1909
Newlands Reclamation Project	March 14, 1903
Nevada National Forest	February 10, 1909
Toiyabe National Forest	February 20, 1909

New Mexico

Alamo National Forest	March 2, 1909
Carlsbad Bird Preserve	February 25, 1909
Carlsbad Reclamation Project	December 2, 1905
Carson National Forest	March 2, 1909
Chaco Canyon National Monument	March 11, 1907
Chiricahua National Forest	July 1, 1908
Datil National Forest	February 23, 1909
El Morro National Monument	December 8, 1906
Gila Cliff Dwellings National Monument	November 16, 1907
Gila National Forest	February 15, 1909
Jemez National Forest	July 1, 1908
Las Animas National Forest	March 1, 1907
Lincoln National Forest	March 2, 1909
Manzano National Forest	April 16, 1908
Pecos National Forest	January 28, 1909
Rio Grande Bird Preserve	February 25, 1909
Rio Grande Reclamation Project	December 2, 1905
Zuni National Forest	March 2, 1909

North Dakota

Chase Lake Bird Preserve	August 28, 1908
Dakota National Forest	November 24, 1908
Lower Yellowstone Reclamation Project	May 10, 1904
Stump Lake Bird Preserve	March 9, 1905
Sullys Hill National Park	June 2, 1904

Oklahoma

Platt National Park	June 29, 1906
Wichita Forest Game Preserve	June 2, 1905
Wichita National Forest	May 29, 1906

Oregon

Boise Reclamation Project	March 27, 1905
Cascade National Forest	July 1, 1908
Cold Springs Bird Preserve	February 25, 1909
Crater Lake National Park	May 22, 1902
Crater National Forest	July 1, 1908
Deschutes National Forest	July 14, 1908
Fremont National Forest	July 14, 1908
Klamath Lake Bird Preserve	August 8, 1908
Klamath National Forest	February 13, 1909
Klamath Reclamation Project	May 15, 1905
Lake Malheur Bird Preserve	August 18, 1908
Malheur National Forest	July 1, 1908
Oregon National Forest	July 1, 1908
Siskiyou National Forest	July 1, 1908
Siuslaw National Forest	July 1, 1908
Three Arch Rocks Bird Preserve	October 14, 1907
Umatilla National Forest	July 1, 1908
Umatilla Reclamation Project	December 4, 1905
Umpqua National Forest	July 1, 1908
Wallowa National Forest	July 1, 1908
Wenaha National Forest	March 1, 1907
Whitman National Forest	July 1, 1908

Puerto Rico

Culebra Bird Preserve	February 27, 1909
Luquillo National Forest	January 17, 1903

South Dakota

Belle Fourche Bird Preserve	February 25, 1909
Belle Fourche Reclamation Project	May 10, 1904
Black Hills National Forest	February 15, 1909
Jewel Cave National Monument	February 7, 1908
Sioux National Forest	February 15, 1909
Wind Cave National Park	January 3, 1903

Utah

Ashley National Forest	July 1, 1908
Cache National Forest	July 1, 1908
Dixie National Forest	February 10, 1909
Fillmore National Forest	July 1, 1908
Fishlake National Forest	July 1, 1908
La Salle National Forest	July 1, 1908
Manti National Forest	April 25, 1907
Minidoka National Forest	July 1, 1908
Natural Bridges National Monument	April 16, 1908
Nebo National Forest	July 1, 1908
Pocatello National Forest	July 1, 1908
Powell National Forest	July 1, 1908
Sevier National Forest	January 17, 1906
Strawberry Valley Bird Preserve	February 25, 1909

Strawberry Valley Reclamation Project	December 15, 1905
Uinta National Forest	July 1, 1908
Wasatch National Forest	July 1, 1908

Washington

Bumping Lake Bird Preserve	February 25, 1909
Chelan National Forest	July 1, 1908
Clealum National Forest	February 25, 1909
Columbia National Forest	July 1, 1908
Colville National Forest	March 1, 1907
Conconuily Bird Preserve	February 25, 1909
Copalis Rock Bird Preserve	October 23, 1907
Flattery Rocks Bird Preserve	October 23, 1907
Kaniksu National Forest	July 1, 1908
Kachess Bird Preserve	February 25, 1909
Keechelus Bird Preserve	February 25, 1909
Mount Olympus National Monument	March 2, 1909
Okanogan Reclamation Project	December 2, 1905
Olympic National Forest	March 2, 1907
Quillayute Needles Bird Preserve	October 23, 1907
Rainer National Forest	July 1, 1908
Snoqualmie National Forest	July 1, 1908
Washington National Forest	July 1, 1908
Wenaha National Forest	March 1, 1907
Wenatchee National Forest	July 1, 1908
Yakima Reclamation Project	December 12, 1905

Wyoming

Ashley National Forest	July 1, 1908
Bighorn National Forest	July 1, 1908
Black Hills National Forest	February 15, 1909
Bonneville National Forest	July 1, 1908
Caribou National Forest	January 15, 1907
Cheyenne National Forest	July 1, 1908
Devils Tower National Monument	September 24, 1906
Hayden National Forest	July 1, 1908
Loch-Katrine Bird Preserve	October 26, 1908
North Platte Reclamation Project	March 14, 1903
Pathfinder Bird Preserve	February 25, 1909
Shoshone Bird Preserve	February 25, 1909
Shoshone National Forest	July 1, 1908
Shoshone Reclamation Project	February 10, 1904
Sundance National Forest	July 1, 1908
Targhee National Forest	July 1, 1908
Teton National Forest	July 1, 1908
Wyoming National Forest	July 1, 1908

Appendix C

How Much Do You Know about Theodore Roosevelt National Park?

There are twenty-five questions on the following quiz. Answers and an assessment tool are available at the end. Have fun!

1. Why did Theodore Roosevelt first come to North Dakota?
   a. To buy cattle ranches
   b. To hunt bison
   c. To hunt grizzly bear
   d. For his job working as a Northern Pacific Railroad foreman
   e. As a U.S. Army colonel posted at Fort Abraham Lincoln

2. What is the fastest land animal you can see in the park (it's also the fastest animal in North America)?
   a. Coyote
   b. Black-footed ferret
   c. Bison
   d. Elk
   e. Pronghorn

3. Which of the following products has an association with a person linked to Medora?
   a. Scotch® tape
   b. Luden's® cough drops
   c. Fanta® soft drinks
   d. Pillsbury® biscuits
   e. Mr. Bubble® bubble bath

4. **Which of the following animals will sometimes team up with a coyote to hunt prairie dogs?**
    a. Badger
    b. Cougar
    c. Bobcat
    d. Black-footed ferret
    e. Golden eagle

5. **Which of the following animals lives in large colonies?**
    a. Prairie dog
    b. Turkey vulture
    c. Cougar
    d. Dung beetle
    e. Badger

6. **The founder of Medora was:**
    a. Harry V. Johnston
    b. The Marquis de Mores
    c. Medora Von Hoffman
    d. E. G. Paddock
    e. Gumbo Lily

7. **During his life, Theodore Roosevelt was NOT which of the following:**
    a. Author
    b. Governor of New York
    c. New York City Police Commissioner
    d. Army colonel
    e. Superintendent of New York City's Central Park

8. **What is the most common type of tree you will see in the park?**
    a. Cottonwood
    b. Green ash
    c. Rocky Mountain juniper
    d. Ponderosa pine
    e. White pine

9. What is the highest point in the park?
   a. Peck Hill
   b. Sperati Point
   c. Buck Hill
   d. Battleship Butte
   e. Johnston Plateau

10. Wildland fires _____ .
   a. Destroy people's homes and property
   b. Can eliminate exotic plants
   c. Attract wildlife in their aftermath
   d. Have been used historically for habitat control, hunting, and warfare
   e. All of the above

11. Tamarisk (salt cedar) is a nonnative plant to the Badlands area and
   a. Produces a milky latex that causes skin irritation
   b. Has thorny spines that discourage animals from eating it
   c. Can use more than 250 gallons of water per day
   d. Brings a companion beetle with it that devastates native grasses
   e. Is loved for its beautiful leaves and picturesque branches

12. The Three Affiliated Tribes of North Dakota are
   a. The Mandan, Hidatsa, and Arikara
   b. The Mandan, Hidatsa, and Sioux
   c. The Crow, Sioux, and Arikara
   d. The Crow, Hidatsa, and Arikara
   e. The Crow, Sioux, and Assiniboin

13. If the Petrified Forest were cut down, it would be worth about $23 million.
   a. True
   b. False

14. **What trail connects all three units of the park?**
    a. The Buffalo Gap Trail
    b. The Maah Daah Hey Trail
    c. The Long X Trail
    d. The Custer Trail
    e. The Roosevelt Trail

15. **Where do you have the chance of seeing bighorn sheep in the park?**
    a. The North Unit
    b. The South Unit
    c. The Elkhorn Ranch
    d. All three units
    e. There are no bighorn sheep in the park

16. **Where do you have the chance of seeing wolves in the park?**
    a. The North Unit
    b. The South Unit
    c. The Elkhorn Ranch
    d. All three units
    e. There are no wolves in the park

17. **Where do you have the chance of seeing wild horses in the park?**
    a. The North Unit
    b. The South Unit
    c. The Elkhorn Ranch
    d. All three units
    e. There are no wild horses in the park

18. **Theodore Roosevelt operated which of the following two ranches?**
    a. The Long X and the Elkhorn
    b. The Three Sevens and the Maltese Cross
    c. Peaceful Valley and the Long X
    d. The Elkhorn and the Maltese Cross
    e. The Three Sevens and the Elkhorn

19. Bison:
   a. Were hunted to near extinction
   b. Bones were at one time made into toothpaste
   c. Live for fifty years on average
   d. Mate in two separate periods each year
   e. All of the above

20. The Long X Trail:
   a. Connects all three units of the park
   b. Was a well-known trail used to drive cattle north
   c. Was partly used by Custer when marching to the Battle of Little Bighorn
   d. Was a trail Theodore Roosevelt used to easily get from one ranch to another
   e. All of the above

21. Fort Union was a trading post and not a military post.
   a. True
   b. False

22. Knife River was where groups of primarily _____ people lived.
   a. Arikara and Hidatsa
   b. Sioux and Crow
   c. Mandan and Sioux
   d. Mandan and Hidatsa
   e. Crow and Arikara

23. In North Dakota you can see:
   a. The "House of Mud"
   b. The Theodore Roosevelt Presidential Library
   c. Theodore Roosevelt's grave
   d. The largest scrap-metal sculptures in the world
   e. The largest man-made lake in the world

24. Theodore Roosevelt National Park is significant because

a. It protects a mixed-grass prairie ecosystem

b. Showcases the unusual, scenic Badlands and their unique history

c. It was a place where Theodore Roosevelt spent time and had experiences that influenced his character and beliefs about conservation

d. Provides visitors with countless recreation opportunities

e. All of the above

25. Roosevelt is known as America's Conservation President because he

a. Created 51 federal bird preserves and 4 wildlife preserves

b. Created 150 national forests and 24 reclamation projects

c. Created 18 national monuments and 5 national parks

d. Protected an estimated 230 million acres of land

e. All of the above

Scoring the Quiz

Theodore Roosevelt believed that a president should use the "bully pulpit" to express his beliefs about what was best for society and pursue an aggressive agenda. The word "bully" was used by Roosevelt as an adjective that expressed an excellent quality to something (think magnificent, wonderful, or awesome). The term is used here for you to assess your level of knowledge about Theodore Roosevelt National Park.

Answers:
1. b 2. e 3. e 4. a 5. a 6. b 7. e 8. c 9. a 10. e 11. c 12. a 13. b 14. b 15. a 16. e 17. b 18. d 19. a 20. b 21. a 22. d 23. d 24. e 25. e

You got _____ questions right. Your knowledge of Theodore Roosevelt National Park is:

0–10	Bullyproof!
11–15	Not so bully
16–20	Bully
21–25	Bully good!

Appendix D
Park Wildlife

These lists are reprinted courtesy of Theodore Roosevelt National Park. Insects and other small animals are too numerous to be included.

Mammals

Order	Common Name	Scientific Name
ARTIODACTYLA (cloven-hoofed)	Wapiti (Elk)	*Cervus elaphus*
	Mule Deer	*Odocoileus hemionus*
	White-tailed Deer	*Odocoileus virginianus*
	Pronghorn (Antelope)	*Antilocapra americana*
	American Bison (Buffalo, Tatanka)— reintroduced	*Bison bison*
	Mountain Sheep (Bighorn Sheep)— reintroduced to replace Audubon bighorn, *O.c. auduboni* now extinct.	*Ovis canadensis californiana*
	Longhorn—introduced— historic demonstration	*Bos taurus*
PERISSODACTYLA (singletoed-hoofed)	Feral Horse (Wild Horse) —introduced—historic demonstration	*Equus caballus*
CARNIVORA (flesh eaters)	Coyote	*Canis latrans*
	Swift Fox—very rare	*Vulpes velox*
	Red Fox—uncommon	*Vulpes vulpes*
	Raccoon—uncommon	*Procyon lotor*

Mammals *(cont'd)*

Order	Common Name	Scientific Name
	Long-tailed Weasel	*Mustela frenata*
	Black-footed Ferret— extirpated	*Mustela nigripes*
	Least Weasel—very rare	*Mustela rixosa*
	Mink	*Mustela vison*
	Badger	*Taxidea taxus*
	Striped Skunk	*Mephitis mephitis*
	River Otter—extirpated	*Lutra canadensis*
	Mountain Lion—rare	*Felis concolor*
	Lynx—very rare	*Felis canadensis*
	Bobcat—uncommon	*Felis rufus*
RODENTIA (gnawing)	Least Chipmunk	*Tamias minimus*
	Richardson's Ground Squirrel—very rare	*Spermophilus richardsonii*
	Thirteen-lined Ground Squirrel	*Spermophilus tridecemlineatus*
	Black-tailed Prairie Dog	*Cynomys ludovicianus*
	Fox Squirrel	*Sciurus niger*
	Northern Pocket Gopher	*Thomomys talpoides*
	Olive-backed Pocket Mouse	*Perognathus fasciatus*
	Ord's Kangaroo Rat	*Dipodomys ordii*
	Beaver	*Caster canadensis*
	Western Harvest Mouse	*Reithrodontomys megalotis*
	White-footed Mouse— uncommon	*Peromyscus leucopus*
	Deer Mouse	*Peromyscus maniculatus*
	Northern Grasshopper Mouse	*Onychomys leucogaster*
	Bushy-tailed Woodrat	*Neotoma cinerea*

Order	Common Name	Scientific Name
	Prairie Vole	*Microtus ochrogaster*
	Meadow Vole	*Microtus pennsylvanicus*
	Sagebrush Vole— uncommon	*Lagurus curtatus*
	Muskrat—rare	*Ondatra zibethicus*
	Meadow Jumping Mouse	*Zapus hudsonius*
	Porcupine	*Erethizon dorsatum*
	House Mouse	*Mus musculus*
LAGOMORPHA (rabbits, hares, pikas)	Desert Cottontail	*Sylvilagus audubonii*
	Eastern Cottontail	*Sylvilagus floridanus*
	Nuttall's Cottontail— very rare	*Sylvilagus nuttallii*
	Snowshoe Hare	*Lepus americanus*
	Prairie Hare (White-tailed Jackrabbit)	*Lepus townsendii*
CHIROPTERA (bats)	Long-eared Myotis— very rare	*Myotis evotis*
	Keen's Myotis— very rare	*Myotis keenii*
	Small-footed Myotis— uncommon	*Myotis leibii*
	Little Brown Myotis	*Myotis lucifugus*
	Long-legged Myotis	*Myotis volans*
	Silver-haired Bat	*Lasionycteris noctivagans*
	Big Brown Bat	*Eptesicus fuscus*
	Red Bat	*Lasiurus borealis*
	Hoary Bat	*Lasiurus cinereus*
INSECTIVORA (shrews, moles)	Masked Shrew—uncommon	*Sorex cinereus*
	Merriam's Shrew	*Sorex merriami*

Reptiles and Amphibians

Order	Common Name	Scientific Name
REPTILES	Common Snapping Turtle	*Chelydra serpentina*
	Western Painted Turtle	*Chrysemys picta*
	Soft-shelled Turtle	*Trionyx muticus*
	Sagebrush Lizard	*Sceloporus graciosus*
	Short-horned Lizard	*Phrynosoma douglassi*
	Western Plains Garter Snake	*Thamnophis radix*
	Red-sided Garter Snake	*Thamnophis sirtalis*
	Western Smooth Green Snake	*Opheodrys vernalis*
	Plains Hognose Snake	*Heterodon nasicus*
	Yellow-bellied (Blue) Racer	*Coluber constrictor*
	Bull snake (Gopher Snake)	*Pituophis melanoleucus*
	Prairie Rattlesnake	*Crotalus viridis*
AMPHIBIANS	Tiger Salamander	*Ambystoma tigrinum*
	Plains Spadefoot Toad	*Scaphiopus bombifrons*
	Great Plains Toad	*Bufo cognatus*
	Rocky Mountain (Woodhouse's) Toad	*Bufo woodhousei*
	Boreal Chorus Frog	*Pseudacris nigrita*
	Leopard Frog	*Rana pipiens*

Fish

Species of fish that live in the portions of the Little Missouri River in the park include carpsuckers, chubs, catfish, goldeyes, minnows, redhorses, and saugers.

Birds

Ask for a bird checklist at one of the park's visitor centers—189 species have been observed in Theodore Roosevelt National Park, and at least 22 more have been seen in nearby areas and are suspected to use the park.

Appendix E
Common Park Plants

The following information and list are reprinted courtesy of Theodore Roosevelt National Park.

This flora list represents 102 of the more common plants found in Theodore Roosevelt National Park. More than 400 plants have been located and identified within the park, and it is estimated that perhaps as many as 500 different species exist here. Please respect other park visitors as well as wildlife when viewing wildflowers. Picking or collecting plants is prohibited by federal law.

Plants listed can be found in one or all three units of the park. Common names shown are those used in this region. Scientific names follow the convention used in *Flora of the Great Plains* (University Press of Kansas, 1986) unless later accepted changes have been made. Flowering date represents the best time to see the plant in bloom under normal conditions. Dates could be altered by weather. Space permits listing only primary habitat.

Grasses

Common Name	Scientific Name	Family	Habitat
Big sandgrass	*Calamovilfa longifolia*	Grass	Sandy setting
Blue grama	*Bouteloua*	Grass	Prairie
Buffalo grass	*Buchloe dactyloides*	Grass	Uplands
Canada wild rye	*Elymus canadensis*	Grass	Riverbottom/ channels
Crested wheatgrass	*Agropyron cristatum*	Grass	Roadsides
Foxtail barley	*Hordeum jubatum*	Grass	Alkaline settings
Green needlegrass	*Stipa viridula*	Grass	Prairie
Junegrass	*Koeleria pyramidata*	Grass	Prairie
Kentucky bluegrass	*Poa pratensis*	Grass	Campground
Little bluestem	*Andropogon scoparius*	Grass	Ridge slopes

Grasses *(cont'd)*

Common Name	Scientific Name	Family	Habitat
Needle-and-thread	*Stipa comata*	Grass	Prairie
Threadleaf sedge	*Carex filifolia*	Sedge	Prairie uplands
Saltgrass	*Distichlis spicata stricta*	Grass	Alkaline settings
Sideoats grama	*Bouteloua curtipendula*	Grass	Ridge slopes
Smooth brome	*Bromus inermis*	Grass	Roadsides
Western wheatgrass (state grass)	*Agropyron smithii*	Grass	Uplands

Shrubs

Common Name	Scientific Name	Family	Flowering Time	Flower Color
Big sage/Three-toothed sage	*Artemisia tridentata*	Aster		
Buckbrush/Wolfberry	*Symphoricarpos occidentalis*	Honeysuckle	June–July	White
Buffaloberry/Bullberry	*Shepherdia argentea*	Oleaster		
Choke cherry	*Prunus virginiana*	Rose	May–June	White
Common/Shrub juniper/cedar	*Juniperus communis*	Cypress		
Creeping juniper/cedar	*Juniperus horizontalis*	Cypress		
Skunkbush/Fragrant sumac	*Rhus aromatica*	Cashew	May–June	Yellow
Golden/Buffalo currant	*Ribes odoratum*	Currant	May	Yellow
Greasewood	*Sarcobatus vermiculatus*	Goosefoot		
Juneberry/Saskatoon	*Amelanchier alnifolia*	Rose		
Poison ivy	*Toxicodendron rydbergii*	Cashew		

Common Name	Scientific Name	Family	Flowering Time	Flower Color
Prairie rose (state flower)	*Rosa arkansana*	Rose	June–July	Pink
Rabbitbrush	*Chrysothamnus nauseosus*	Aster	Aug–Sept	Yellow
Sandbar willow	*Salix interior*	Willow		
Shrubby cinquefoil/ Potentilla	*Potentilla fruiticosa*	Rose	June–Aug	Yellow
Silver sage	*Artemisia cana*	Aster		
Spiny saltbush	*Atriplex confertiflora*	Goosefoot		
Wild plum	*Prunus americana*	Rose	May	White
Winterfat	*Ceratoides lanata*	Goosefoot		
Wood's rose	*Rosa woodsii*	Rose	June	Pink

Trees

Common Name	Scientific Name	Family	Habitat
American elm	*Ulmus americana*	Elm	Riverbottom/ draws
Box elder	*Acer negundo*	Maple	Riverbottom
Cottonwood	*Populus deltoides*	Willow	Riverbottom
Green ash	*Fraxinus pennsylvanica*	Olive	Draws/ riverbottom
Rocky Mountain juniper/cedar	*Juniperus scopulorum*	Cypress	North-facing slopes

Herbs

Common Name	Scientific Name	Family	Flowering Time	Flower Color
Aromatic aster	*Aster oblongifolius*	Aster	Aug–Sept	Purple
Bastard toadflax	*Comandra umbellata*	Sandalwood	May–June	White
Bergamot/Beebalm	*Monarda fistulosa*	Mint	July–Aug	Pink

Herbs *(cont'd)*

Common Name	Scientific Name	Family	Flowering Time	Flower Color
Blazing star/Dotted gayfeather	*Liatris aspera*	Aster	Aug–Sept	Purple
Blue wild lettuce	*Lactuca oblongifolia*	Aster	June–Sept	Purple
Butte candle	*Cryptantha celosioides*	Borage	June	White
Common sunflower	*Helianthus annuus*	Aster	July–Sept	Yellow
Crested beardtongue	*Penstemon eriantherus*	Figwort	June	Purple
Crocus/Pasque flower	*Anemone patens*	Buttercup	April–June	Purple
Curlycup gumweed	*Grindelia squarrosa*	Aster	July–Sept	Yellow
False Solomon's seal	*Smilacina stellata*	Lily	June	White
Fetid marigold	*Dyssodia papposa*	Aster	June–Aug	Yellow
Field bindweed	*Convolvulus sepium*	Morning Glory	June–July	White
Fringed sage	*Artemisia frigida*	Aster	Aug–Sept	Yellowish
Goat's beard/ Western salsify	*Tragopogon dubius*	Aster	June–Aug	Yellow
Golden aster	*Chrysopsis villosa*	Aster	July–Sept	Yellow
Golden pea	*Thermopsis rhombifolia*	Pea	May–June	Yellow
Goldenrod	*Solidago spp.*	Aster	Aug–Sept	Yellow
Ground plum	*Astragalus crassicarpus*	Bean	May–June	Pink
Gumbo lily	*Oenothera caespitosa*	Primrose	June	White
Harebell	*Campanula rotundifolia*	Bellflower	June–July	Purple
Henbane	*Hyoscamus niger*	Potato	June	Greenish
Indian breadroot/ Tipsin	*Psoralea esculenta*	Pea	May–June	Purple
Indian paintbrush	*Castilleja sessiliflora*	Figwort	May–July	Yellow
Large-flowered dock	*Rumex venosus*	Buckwheat	May–June	Pink
Leafy spurge	*Euphorbia esula*	Spurge	June–July	Greenish
Leopard lily	*Fritillaria atropurpurea*	Lily	May	Purple

Common Name	Scientific Name	Family	Flowering Time	Flower Color
Moss phlox	*Phlox hoodii*	Phlox	May–June	White
Northern bedstraw	*Galium boreale*	Madder	June–July	White
Pincushion cactus	*Coryphantha vivipara*	Cactus	June	Red
Prickly pear cactus	*Opuntia polyacantha*	Cactus	June	Yellow
Prince's plume	*Stanleya pinnata*	Mustard	June	Yellow
Purple coneflower	*Echinacea augustifolia*	Aster	June–July	Purple
Purple locoweed	*Oxytropis lambertii*	Pea	May–July	Purple
Purple prairie clover	*Dalea purpurea*	Pea	July	Purple
Pussytoes	*Antennaria spp.*	Aster	June	White
Rocky Mountain bee plant	*Cleome serrulata*	Caper	June–Sept	Pink
Sago/Mariposa lily	*Calochortus nuttallii*	Lily	June–July	White
Scarlet gaura	*Gaura coccinea*	Primrose	May–Aug	White/red
Scarlet/ Red globe mallow	*Sphaeralcea coccinea*	Mallow	June–Sept	Red
Scoria lily/ Evening star	*Mentzelia decapetala*	Stickleaf	July–Aug	White
Showy milkweed	*Asclepias speciosa*	Milkweed	June–Aug	Pink
Silver-leaf scurf pea	*Psoralea argophylla*	Pea	June–Sept	Purple
Skeletonweed	*Lygodesmia juncea*	Aster	June–Sept	Pink
Snakeweed	*Gutierrezia sarothrae*	Aster	Aug–Sept	Yellow
Spreading dogbane	*Apocynum androsaemifolium*	Dogbane	June–July	White
Stiff sunflower	*Helianthus rigidus*	Aster	Aug–Sept	Yellow
Tumbling mustard	*Sisymbrium altissimum*	Mustard	June–Aug	Yellow
Wavy-leaf thistle	*Circium undulatum*	Aster	June–July	Purple
Western virgin's bower	*Clematis ligusticifolia*	Buttercup	July–Aug	White
Western wallflower	*Erysimum asperum*	Mustard	May–July	Yellow
White beardtongue/ penstemon	*Penstemon albidus*	Figwort	June–July	White

Herbs *(cont'd)*

Common Name	Scientific Name	Family	Flowering Time	Flower Color
White sage	*Artemisia ludoviciana*	Aster		
White sweet clover	*Melilotus alba*	Pea	June–July	White
White wild onion/ Prairie onion	*Allium textile*	Lily	May–June	White
Whorled milkweed	*Asclepias verticillata*	Milkweed	July–Aug	White
Wild licorice	*Glycyrrhiza lepidota*	Pea	June	Yell/white
Wooly plantain	*Plantago patagonica*	Plaintain	June	
Yarrow	*Achillea millefolium*	Aster	June–July	White
Yellow buckwheat/ umbrella plant	*Eriogonum flavum*	Buckwheat	May–July	Yellow
Yucca	*Yucca glauca*	Lily	June	White

Index

About the Author

When people heard that Levi Novey planned on taking his park ranger work so seriously that he was going to take a job at an obscure national park in North Dakota, they were more than a little bit curious. After all, North Dakota is a place that remains more shrouded in mystery than any other state in the United States. By accepting the job, Levi experienced what it was like to pick up a bison "chip," release a captive bull snake only to watch it seek imprisonment again, sit near a bugling elk while seeing the Northern Lights for the first  time, and have more memorable hiking trips than anywhere else he has ever worked or played. Essentially he learned what makes Theodore Roosevelt National Park sing to the hearts of its visitors.

Levi is a conservation professional and has received a bachelor's degree in History from Tufts University and a master's degree in Conservation Social Sciences from the University of Idaho. He has worked for six national parks as a park ranger and as a researcher for five others. He has taught an undergraduate Environmental Communication Skills course at the University of Idaho, won several photography contests, and regularly enjoys visits to parks, protected areas, historical sites, museums—and just about anywhere where he can learn something new about the world. He and his wife, Alicia, currently live in Moscow, Idaho.

If you would like to reach Levi, or have suggestions for future editions of this book, send an e-mail to levi.novey@gmail.com.

Outfit Your Mind

falcon.com